Stand Up
or
Sit Out

*Memories and Musings of a Blind Wrestler,
Runner, and All-Around Regular Guy*

Anthony R. Candela

ISBN 978-1-0980-0566-5 (paperback)
ISBN 978-1-0980-0567-2 (digital)

Copyright © 2019 by Anthony R. Candela

All rights reserved. No part of this publication may be reproduced, distributed, or transmitted in any form or by any means, including photocopying, recording, or other electronic or mechanical methods without the prior written permission of the publisher. For permission requests, solicit the publisher via the address below.

Christian Faith Publishing, Inc.
832 Park Avenue
Meadville, PA 16335
www.christianfaithpublishing.com

Printed in the United States of America

Contents

Acknowledgments 5
Prologue 9
Introduction 13
Beginnings 17
Young Jock 37
Kelly Green and White 59
Interlude 74
Into the Deep 84
Approaching the Run 97
Achilles and the Marathon 119
How the Race Is Run 136
Triathlon Man 154
Coming Home 170
Ages of a Man 181
Resolution 203
Epilogue 211
References 215

Acknowledgments

It takes lots of support to publish a memoir. Many thanks go to Jordyn and the entire family of editors, illustrators and other highly skilled professionals at Christian Faith Publishing who cradled my labor of love as if it were their own.

Of course, had my parents, Joseph and Catherine, not brought me into the world, none of these words or any of the experiences behind them would have been written. They watched me grow from an undoubtedly vexing infant into an equally mysterious adult, braving consternation and guilt at times, and hopefully pride at others. My brothers, Lenny and Joseph, whose lives I have watched both parallel and diverge from my own, deserve kudos for enduring the unwanted competition that occasionally comes when one has an older brother and for continuing to be a part of my team. Although we lived on opposite coasts for sixteen years while they assumed the bulk of the responsibility for assisting our parents to maintain an independent and quality life, brothers are brothers forever, and they appear to have forgiven me for having succumbed to wanderlust.

The teachers and coaches who shepherded me through green and not-so-green pastures deserve my eternal gratitude. To Mr. Mercurio, who introduced me to wrestling in elementary school; Coaches McGuire and Daniels, my high school junior varsity and varsity wrestling coaches, respectively; and Dr. Bennet, who coached me through my college years—thank you.

Joe Casarella was an avid supporter in my high school years. Although a football coach and later the athletic director, for some reason, which I can only attribute to his appreciation of athletic effort, especially from one with a disability, he took an interest in me. Thanks, Coach!

To the open-minded scuba instructors from a local dive shop in Yonkers, New York, whose names I've long-since forgotten, your willingness to take a chance on a severely visually impaired student when you had never seen one before will be forever appreciated. You taught me how to breathe underwater, to calculate "bottom time" before digital diving watches made it easier, and of course, to enjoy effortless movement in three-dimensional space.

It was the Moray Wheels, a disability-oriented diving club from Boston, that gave me the widest variety of opportunities to descend to the depths. Ironically, the best dive of all was the shallowest—a ten-foot descent into a tank at the Boston Aquarium. It provided the kind of intimate experience with creatures of the deep most humans can only approximate from outside a wall of glass.

Similarly, the Alpine ski instructors of the BOLD (Blind Outdoor Leisure Development) program assisted me to crash barriers that have prevented many blind people from even dreaming of mounting and dismounting a ski lift, no less rapidly and skillfully edging their way down steep and turning slopes of hard-packed snow, hard-wooded trees, and hard-to-ignore precipices. Likewise, the folks at Sierra Regional Ski for Light, a cross-country skiing program for blind persons, provided me a chance to get back on the slopes in California well after my downhill career had ended.

Many thanks go to the running and cycling partners who, through the years, enabled me to get out there and pound the pavement. To Sharon, Adria, Kay, Amy, and Mary—thank you. Mike, Jeff, and Robby—you are the best. Special thanks go to my physical therapists, Harriet and Dennis Surdi, and my wonderful podiatrist, the late Dr. Murray Weisenfeld, for patching me up every time I sustained a running injury. To the late Fred Lebow and the New York Road Runners Club, the Achilles Track Club, the Van Cortlandt Track Club, and the New York Central Park Triathlon—thank you for taking me under your wings and into your hearts.

My fondest gratitude is reserved for my first and only running coach, Dick Traum. Thank you, Dick, for encouraging me to run, for creating the Achilles Track Club, and for your service to people with disabilities around the world.

To the Big Brothers, Big Sisters of America, the *New York Times*, the *Rockland Journal News*, and WABC TV in New York—thanks for the honors and publicity!

Without my work, life would be incomplete. Since time immemorial, people with disabilities have endured nearly 70 percent unemployment and underemployment. Although today, those of us lucky and skillful enough to secure jobs rely upon assistive technologies to perform our duties to maximum efficiency; occasionally, human assistance is necessary. This was certainly the case more than forty years ago when I commenced my career as a Vocational Rehabilitation Counselor. Bob, my longtime reader and friend, wherever you are, I know God smiles upon you. In your time, you endured war and prejudice and came through it one of the finest men I've ever known.

Although I treasure all my relationships, one in particular requires mentioning here. In 2002, two and a half years after we parted, my second wife, Jamie, passed away, a victim of breast cancer. She lived her life to the fullest and, I was told, held her head high through the fear and suffering that accompanies this malady.

Thanks go to Heller, my first steady jogging partner when I landed in California in 2000. She allowed me to bore her with reminiscences and trusted me to nudge her past points of pain and keep her wanting to return to the track.

Words are not enough to thank my partner for seven years in the 2000s—Cathy, the woman who inspired me to greater intellectual heights than I might have tried to reach on my own, and hence, this memoir. Her gentle and steadfast personality was matched only by her intellectual acumen. An academic and excellent writer in her own right, she guided, advised, and kept me whole through the arduous work necessary to complete the first draft.

Lest I forget, thank you to everyone else who read various drafts of this work. Your contributions to my thinking and demands that I not settle for second best were invaluable.

Prologue

The quarter-mile track at Berkeley's Martin Luther King Junior High School surrounds a soccer field always buzzing with activity. A small group of neighborhood grown-ups, my friend and I among them, go there to jog. There is a specially planted garden adjacent to the track, inspired by Alice Waters, world-famous advocate for farmers markets and for sound and sustainable agriculture. Prince Charles and Camilla have even visited this place. On any given morning or late afternoon, neighborhood kids, ranging in age from eight to thirteen, gather with their parent-coaches (soccer moms and dads all) to learn how to run, kick, dribble, and score.

Their excited voices waft to our ears. We are on the outside of a scene we would dearly love to join, but whose boundaries we dare not penetrate. We adults have already been molded; our attitudes toward sports, competition, and life itself unalterable at this late date. Or are they? The children affect us. Their voices paint a beneficent glow upon our faces. Intermingled with exhortations and encouragement from the adults, the children's utterances strike us as innocent, devoid of care, and full of promise.

The mood is pleasant. Here in laid-back Northern California, parents and coaches seem especially aware of the importance of teaching young athletes how to work as a team. No one scolds them for losing the ball or missing a shot on goal. Ignoring a passing opportunity might raise a few eyebrows. After all, cooperation and combined effort is what teamwork is all about. Unperturbed, the children laugh, grunt with the genuine effort they seem to put into their game, and encourage each other with gusto. It is the year 2000, and I've just arrived here from New York. I am forty-seven years old.

My friend and I jog slowly around the track. "Let's try to run today's mile in eleven minutes," I suggest. She hesitantly agrees. "It's been a week since we last ran. I hope I can do it," she says.

We circumnavigate the activity. I listen intently to the children playing, and it occurs to me that I have been given a gift. I am privileged to watch, as if through a rose-colored time portal, my own development as a competitive individual. Only it is not the past I am watching. It is the present, an altered version of what might have been. Here, in real time, the children's attitudes toward competition and achievement are being molded. They are about the same age as I was when I first learned how to compete. When these children grow up, I wonder, what kind of attitude toward athletics will they have? How will they react the first time someone tells them their performance wasn't good enough to win? How will they handle defeat, or victory, for that matter? How will this affect their lives?

We finish our four laps and are done for the day. "Eleven minutes," I announce. Nice job.

My friend catches her breath as we walk away from the track. "Thanks for putting up with me," she gasps. "This must be boring for you."

My friend and I have run together, three or four times per week, for the better part of the time I've lived in Northern California. She has been forced to listen to my stories about the glory days, nearly a decade ago, when I was a long-distance runner. As we run, she can tell that my body hasn't forgotten how to glide smoothly and effortlessly across long distances. She knows that the three or four miles a week that we run together would have been a mere warm-up for me back then. "No," I answer. "I'm happy to run with you. Many good runners have done the same for me."

"Why don't you run more?" she presses. You can run more after almost a decade of being away from racing than I'll ever be able to run."

"I know what will happen," I assert. "The adrenalin will start flowing, my distances will increase, my times will drop, and the next thing you know, I'll want to start competing. I'm not sure if I want to go there again."

"Surely, there's a middle ground." Although true, it doesn't always work that way. If I'd been introduced to sports like the children in the soccer field, I muse, perhaps I'd be mellower. I could conceivably find a way to work hard, have fun, stay injury-free, and become only a little competitive.

Just then I hear one of the soccer dads yell, "Come on. Run harder. Don't be a wimp. They're beating you."

"Oh well," I muttered, "I guess it really is an imperfect world. Who's to say what is right and what is wrong?"

Turning to look at the children's reaction, my friend observes, "Some of them seem to be running harder. They have smiles on their faces. Others are moping along. That's sad."

A soccer mom calls out, "Do your best, kids. Have fun."

"There you have it," I laughed, "the ying and the yang."

My friend quips incisively, "You've certainly gone California!"

Introduction

Some people are sprinters, some run marathons, and most fall in between. They are the special ones, the ones who compete but never make the headlines. They are most like you and me.

When I began writing this memoir, I thought it would simply be a cathartic endeavor. I didn't consider publishing it until friends reminded me that the object of my explorations—to make sense of my life and transmit my discoveries to others—is why we write memoirs. The basic task of all human beings, in my opinion, is to find harmony between our fundamental imperfections and demands for high performance placed upon us by the environment within which we live. Call it "man against nature," "social Darwinism," or the "Adam and Eve" creation myth, every day, we who live in society face pressures to function both within and outside our basic nature. While we are taught to sublimate selfish impulses, we are encouraged (especially in Western cultures) to excel and separate ourselves from the pack. Freedom to fulfill our potential brings with it the burden to live within a duality. We are often asked to reach for the stars while keeping our feet planted firmly on the ground. It is these elements that I hope my athletic adventures and introspections will illustrate.

Certainly, my effort to excel in sports pushed me to function both within and outside my own nature. I hope, even if the specific aspects of the sports I describe are not interesting to everyone, their capacity to widen one's horizons will be evident to all. And who knows? My descriptions might titillate someone's fancy. The vignettes may inspire a few readers to try a little wrestling, a bit of running, a cycling trip, a dip in the swimming pool, a dabble in downhill skiing or a Nordic trek, or a dive into the deep blue sea.

In the early 1970s, while walking on campus with two members of my college wrestling team, a young man with an athletic build greeted one of my companions. They appeared to know each other from their high school days. As we continued on our way, my teammate informed us that the fellow was probably the best wrestler that would ever grace our campus. "Why wasn't he a member of our team?" I asked. "He's burned out," stated my friend. "In high school, he pushed himself so hard to become a state champion that he doesn't want anything more to do with competitive sports."

I wondered if the achievement had been worth the price. Then I recalled one of my own high school wrestling teammates. An excellent athlete, a "two-letter man," he dropped off the wrestling team after making the varsity the previous two years when, due to fatigue, he failed to win the first match of his senior year. Apparently, he had lost more weight than his body could easily tolerate. We never saw him on the mats again.

This reminder of the frailty of even the most physically tough among us stayed with me. In the pages that follow, I hope the fruits of my own experiences with these two sides of our psyches will make for an easy and fun-filled read. Written for the athletic and nonathletic reader, the legacy I hope this memoir leaves is awareness of the elements of sport, the attraction it has for so many of us, and the care we must take to make sure it remains enjoyable.

The decision to publish this memoir proved to be as tough a feat as any wrestling match or road race in which I ever competed. Once I convinced myself to share my story, putting the words on paper (to use an anachronism in the digital age) became a labor of love. The long trek of remembrance, research, reminiscence, and reconstruction now nestles comfortably in the same warm place in my memories as those you will read about on the following pages.

Going public with these musings was a difficult choice. The difficulty stems from a tradition I learned from my fellow athletes. In this tradition, one learns the importance of balancing exhibitionism with humility. This message was brought home to me one day in high school. While standing in a hallway with a group of fellow wrestlers, I decided to show off my biceps. Since I wore a short-sleeved shirt, they were easily visible when I flexed them. Stepping in front of me, a burly teammate punched me hard in the chest. I thought I was going to pass out. After recovering, I demanded to know why he had struck me. His words, "We don't show off," permeate my life to this day, much as the memory of that punch still resonates within my chest!

Some of my reservations about publicity stem from perspectives I developed as a person with a disability. Popular culture tends to view stories about people with disabilities in two different ways: transcendence or catastrophe. Thankful for their faculties, people without disabilities unconsciously worry that serious disability could be a part of their futures. As the expression goes, "There but for the grace of God go I." These readers want to be left with good feelings. They want to know that calamitous as a situation may seem, there is hope that things will all work out in the end. They prefer, for example, stories depicting a blind person as a hero, overcoming all odds—a daredevil. This is transcendence.

Most "able-bodied" people view disability as a catastrophe. This is the flip side of transcendence. The basis of this deep-seated belief stems from observations of how people with disabilities exist within and are treated by society. These observations reinforce stereotype and imagination. They believe that people with disabilities must necessarily live miserable lives. Most of us don't think that if society and the environment were kinder, disability would be less difficult. The fundamental belief in catastrophe explains why stories of transcendence have so much impact. After all, the logic goes if you start from a position of incapacity or low expectations, any accomplishment appears wonderful.

I hope the descriptions of my accomplishments will not feed any stereotypes. Instead, I hope my story will cause readers to put down this book and say, "Of course. I can see how he did that" and "I can understand why he didn't do that."

While people with disabilities may have more obstacles than others, neither the obstacles nor the unhappiness are fixed or permanent. This reality is well worth promulgating, and that is why I have chosen to publish these memories.

In writing this memoir, I have tried to depict both the transcendence and catastrophe in my own life. However, I have concluded that there is a third side—"normalcy" or "ordinariness." This might represent the most important aspect of all. Unlike the heroes of stories of transcendence or catastrophe, my life, as it turns out, is more like the lives of the average reader. If I manage to transmit this message, then I will have done the most important thing I can do.

Thus this rendering of my experience is for those who believe that everyday people, living everyday lives, can find happiness—even occasional glory—amidst their trials and tribulations. It can be summed up as a perpetual wrestling match. On one side of the mat, dressed in red, stands human limitations. In the green, on the opposite side of the mat, facing off and ready to spring into action, stands human strivings. We are, after all, imperfect beings, doing our best to be a little less imperfect.

I learned this, most notably, through sports. For those who choose to compete, the "thrill of victory" and the "agony of defeat" can come swiftly—well, perhaps with one exception. Long-distance running, including the marathon, the crème de la crème, delivers its wisdom much more slowly. For those who stay the course and absorb the wisdom written in between the lines of this memoir, the lessons learned will surely strengthen you to your core.

Beginnings

> Harry Truman, Doris Day, Red
> China, Johnny Ray
> South Pacific, Walter Winchell, Joe DiMaggio
> Joe McCarthy, Richard Nixon,
> Studebaker, Television
> North Korea, South Korea, Marilyn Monroe…
>
> —Billy Joel, "We didn't Start the Fire"
> From *Storm Front*, 1989

My parents were "Depression children" and part of the "Greatest Generation." They survived inconceivable fears created by economic disaster and a world war. It was a time when everyone's life was either put on hold or prematurely ended. They emerged to begin a new life, but they did not emerge unscathed. The residue of the era continued to rumble within the depths of their psyches. My generation received the detritus of their trauma and the blessings of their triumphs.

The wars did not end. I was conceived amidst another war, a "police action" in Korea and born just as the conflict ended. Then the Cold War heated up, and a new kind of paranoia gripped my parents' generation, and mine too. The decade of the fifties was also a time of innocence and simplicity. For the most part, gender roles and other "old values" remained intact. The nation completed its highway system, suburbia came into its own, and young people built lives they thought would remain stable.

For many, it was the beginning of a period that left as its legacy a culture in a state of perpetual unease. They transmitted this angst to their progeny. As a result, the generation into which I was born finds itself in the schizophrenic position of craving motion, feeling restless if made to sit still for too long, and yet desiring the familiarity and safety of old habits. We are the baby boomers.

My particular situation was complicated by an added factor: slow loss of eyesight and eventual blindness. It forced me to slow down when I would rather speed up, examine myself when I would rather power my way through stress, compromise when I would rather dominate. Both trauma and triumph became a routine part of my life, and I had to face them from the base of what my parents taught me. As a baby boomer, I inherited the ambiguities of their lives: a deep-seated belief that the world should be predictable and knowable, but tainted by empirical data that said otherwise. Hence, I commenced my journey hesitantly, confused by my parents' bewilderment, driven by their instinct to survive, and hopeful that the modern era would bring with it my deliverance.

I attempted to deal with my confusion through athletics. This effort proved to be, on balance, a success. Of course, with every difficult endeavor comes some failure and disappointment. I may not have always liked what I found, but because of the roads I ran and the problems with which I grappled, I certainly know a lot more about myself and the human condition.

Early Migrations

In 1953, the year of my birth, my parents and I lived in Astoria, Queens, located on the northwestern end of Long Island. The apartment, nestled in a quiet side street near Steinway, a street named after the great piano-making family, did not etch itself into my memory until well after we moved away and returned to visit relatives still living in the area.

Astoria, originally settled by the Dutch in 1637 and incorporated into a village in 1839, had, by 1953, grown into a dynamic, multiethnic section of New York City. Lots of Italian Americans lived there. Later, Greeks and Asians firmly placed their stamp upon the area.

STAND UP OR SIT OUT

My mother, just twenty years old, wheeled me, her firstborn, in a stroller to a nearby park. She learned quickly that parenting is a complex business. For example, she found out that teething can be painful—not only for her young child, but also for the occasional playmate that he nipped with his newly forming dentition. Apparently, signs of my aggressive athletic personality emerged early. I was a biter. More than one playmate was reported to have needed rescuing after my apparent attempts to cannibalize small pieces of their anatomy. Fortunately for them, and for me, the behavior quickly abated, disappearing not too long after it emerged. I have long since switched from those occasional masticatory samplings to a more enjoyable compulsion to devour any dessert treat that comes within range. My sweet tooth has served me well, and my competitive instinct remains. At various times in my life, I have been known to challenge someone to a wrestling match, a race down a snowy mountainside, a ten-mile run, or a good hard swim. A modest athletic achiever, my record is much better when it comes to sweets. Through the years, I have remained confident that no cake, pie, or bowl of ice cream can escape my conquering designs.

My mother grew up in Sicily in the 1930s. Her earliest memories include orderliness and uniformity in all aspects of her young life. Dictated by Mussolini, schools provided quality education (she recalls learning to speak the "high Italian" in contradistinction to the Sicilian dialect spoken in the small villages strewn throughout the island and that the children all wore uniforms). Commerce appeared to proceed in rhythmic fashion, and there was always food on the table, albeit from today's standards, probably not as much as they needed, according to my mother's memory of how much they relied on pasta (carbo-loading). Notwithstanding, life was predictable—that is, until World War II shattered not only the world my mother lived in but the trusting image she had of it. By the time my mother was ten years old (1943), her father had died of an illness, and American soldiers occupied her school. She recalls seeing airplane "dogfights" over the harbor at Palermo some fifteen miles away and wondering if these nice men who gave her candy (including the first African Americans she had ever seen) were the same ones who had terrified her with those aerial displays. She even refused to eat fish until she was certain it didn't come from the waters off Palermo where she knew dead fliers now lay.

My mother also recalls marveling at the flour the Americans provided them. It rendered loaves of bread three times larger than the flour the Italians used. Unfortunately, their airiness made them only a third as filling!

The immense disruption of the war affected my mother's sense of security. I believe she transmitted to me the "background anxiety" she absorbed during those terrible times. We hold in common a sense of worry about things that might happen, guilt about confrontation, and acute sensitivity to the feelings of others. My exaggerated need for security and stability probably comes from my mother. So does my empathy and compassion. Despite the fears and disruption of the Second World War, my mother retained an amazing capacity for finding the good in all people. The gifts she gave me made my eventual selection of the helping professions (counseling, psychology) a natural career choice.

Immigrating to New York in 1947, my mother's attempt to return to school was thwarted by her poor English skills. She went to work in a factory, met and married my father at age eighteen, and two years later became a stay-at-home mom. She would return to work twenty-five years later, after discharging all of her child-rearing duties.

The story of how my mother and father met explains an unusual tie between my siblings and me and our closest cousins. After the war ended, my mother and older brother Sal were left in charge of their youngest brother John while her mother and second youngest brother, Tony, boarded a ship for New York. She, Sal, and John joined them a few months later.

Since for generations many Sicilians had immigrated to the same neighborhoods in New York City, it was no coincidence that my grandmother found an apartment near where my father's (second-generation Sicilian American) family lived. Eventually, my uncle Sal met my father's youngest sister, Catherine, and they began dating. Months later, my father, home on leave from the Marines, met my mother, and they also began dating. Both couples married, and began their families a few months apart from each other. I was the first of my generation; my cousin Marianne entered the world three months later.

These "cross marriages" rendered our extended family smaller as my cousins by Sal and Catherine share both sets of grandparents with my brothers and me. It also caused my cousins to be as genetically close to my brothers and me as they could be without actually being our siblings. This proved important when it was discovered that my eye condition was hereditary. Until the exigencies of time caused us to drift apart, our families were very close.

In 1954, joining a migration trend, my family and I moved to Rockland County and the old Dutch town of Haverstraw, approximately forty miles northwest of the city. Known for its abundance of clay- and the brick-making jobs that came with it in the nineteenth and early twentieth centuries, workers traveled from as far as New York City to work there. Legend has it that on their way home each evening, they tarried to quaff a draft or two in Tarrytown, across the river and southeast of Haverstraw. Tarrytown is next door to Sleepy Hollow, a village made famous by Washington Irving.

We lived in Haverstraw for only a year and then abruptly returned to Astoria. Years later, when I asked why, my father reminded me that the reason was to be closer to doctors who knew about my eye condition and schools with properly trained teachers. The short time we spent in Haverstraw would have faded into insignificance, except that nearly thirty-five years later, I would encounter the then six-year old daughter of a friend of my Uncle Sal. Although I was too young to remember her, she would remember me—and tell about it at a very special occasion.

The Condition

While in Haverstraw, and some months before my third birthday, my parents noticed a tendency that alarmed them. They observed me bumping into objects just on the edge of my path while toddling around the house. Visits to several doctors yielded a diagnosis of retinitis pigmentosa (RP), a genetic condition the doctors said would eventually cause me to lose all my sight. Although there are variations, the type of RP I was born with immediately deprives the owner of peripheral vision, leaving him with "tunnel vision," the ability to see only straight ahead. That explained why I bumped into objects that lay just outside my visual field.

Reeling from a double whammy (not only was their child visually impaired and might go blind, but their combined contribution to my genome might have caused the calamity), my parents tried to cope. Still only in their early twenties, they attempted to fight off the guilt and spring into action. Before finding the doctor who would monitor and attempt to treat my eye condition for the next eighteen years, my parents did what most parents in their situation do: they ran me from doctor to doctor.

"Retinitis pigmentosa." Dr. Bonocolto, the most expert doctor on the condition in New York City at the time, and a grumpy man with an Italian accent, was not the first to offer these words of explanation to my parents for why their firstborn child was bumping into objects. Then came the shattering follow-up. "I believe he will be blind by the time he is an adult." Like hearing a gavel slam after the judge pronounces sentence and the jury goes home, my parents, resigned to the injustice meted out, carried me from the office, determined to make the best of the situation.

I have an autosomal recessive form of RP. Vision deteriorates slowly over a period of years, diminishing to "light perception" by the midforties. There are other genetic types, including autosomal dominant and sex-linked. Some forms of RP allow vision to last longer. Others, such as "Usher syndrome," include deafness or hearing loss. Thankfully, my hearing is intact.

Throughout my childhood, I took vitamin A and D supplements in a vain attempt to slow the progress of the RP. Today, major biomolecular research is attempting to isolate and influence the genetic structure itself in the hopes of preventing the condition or, more ambitiously, stopping or even reversing its course. Some researchers hope healthy retinal cells can be grown and implanted where others have died. Another group leans toward implantation of electronic chips in the retina and brain as a way of circumventing damaged parts and restoring vision. There is much work to be done before any of these approaches will affect regular people in everyday life.

One of the trickiest parts of living with RP is the quality of one's remaining vision. Except for the inability to see in dim or dark places and a corresponding sensitivity to glare, reading is possible well into one's adulthood. Problems arise from imperceptible loss of visual efficiency over time. Due to the slowness of the deterioration, it is easy to develop an amazing capacity to delude one's self into thinking he can still see well. For example, my ability to read (I won awards in first and second grade reading contests) made it easy to decide that learning braille could be put off to the future. This was erroneous thinking. Had I learned to read braille as a child, I would be able to read much faster today. Other than my inability to carry a tune (no relation to RP as far as I know), one of my biggest regrets in life is my slow braille reading speed.

My tunnel vision was even more insidious. How does one know that he doesn't have a full visual field? Since all I could ever do was to see straight ahead, I literally didn't know that I did not possess side vision. I had to be told and then taught to understand. It wasn't until around my ninth or tenth year that I finally got it.

Instinctively, I knew that unless I looked down and made special effort to scan right and left, I would bump into objects or lose sight of the path of a ball rolling on the ground. In fact, my efforts to chase rolling balls were the key to my realizing that other children could see peripherally. A friend, noticing that I often could not find a ball lying nearby, asked me why. I told him because I didn't see it. He told me that, in contrast, he was able to keep his eye on a moving ball with no difficulty. When I told him I had to move my eyes and head to do so, he said if a ball lay a bit to the left or right, he could still see it. I explained that I had to look for the ball if it were not directly where I was facing. That's when it dawned on me that "normal" people had peripheral vision.

"What do you see out to the sides?" my friend asked.

"Nothing, I see as much as I see and then nothing," I answered.

I realized, at a level of sophistication most people never experience, that normal vision must have similar limits. Amazement set in. People see as far to the sides or up and down as they see, and then they simply see nothing more. The term *tunnel vision* is a misnomer. In a tunnel, you can see the sides. In "tunnel vision," you can't. Vision just comes to an end much as it does for people with full visual fields. As far as I know, no one claims that they can see the edge of their eye socket at the border of their peripheral vision!

Still on the Move

In the mid-1950s, my father and uncle took over a diner called the Frying Dutchman to try their hand at keeping it afloat. Their sojourn into the restaurant business ended quickly when, a year later, the diner sinking fast, they disposed of it. The doctor search having ended with my parents settling on Dr. Bonocolto, thoughts turned to where I would go to school.

Surveying the state of the public schools in suburban Haverstraw in 1955, my father felt that New York City might have a better educational system for a visually impaired child. He had heard of two schools for the blind in the Bronx, but his image of what they were like carried an asylum-like tinge. His own school memories included the "sight conservation" teachers he observed working with "special" students. Since the Haverstraw education system had not yet contracted with one of these "special" itinerant teachers, my parents concluded that a strategic return to the city would be best. Since my father often quipped that Marines never retreat; they attack in the opposite direction, we moved back to Astoria.

My father was born and raised on East Sixty-third Street in Manhattan. His mother was born (coincidentally) in Haverstraw and migrated to New York as a young woman. In the early 1900s, his father emigrated from Sicily and ran a candy store in New York City for many years.

As a young boy, my father recalls street fights with the Irish kids, swimming in the East River, playing sandlot baseball, going to Yankees games, joining the Sea Scouts, and wanting to become a chef. Believing cooking to be a feminine occupation, my grandfather forced him to attend automobile mechanics school instead.

In 1947, perhaps partly to achieve independence, my father dropped out of high school and joined the Marine Corps and following his star, became a cook. Rising to sergeant, he was busted to corporal for nearly assaulting a superior officer. The officer had refused to grant him leave to be at his mother's bedside when she died. My father was not yet twenty-one years of age when he lunged and missed the officer with what, given his profound pain, would surely have been a devastating punch.

In 1951, after an honorable discharge, my father, along with thousands of other reservists, was recalled to the Marines when the Korean conflict broke out. While preparing to ship out to Korea, he severely injured his back, was hospitalized, and discharged with a disability designation. Over the next twenty years, he would undergo more than fifteen major back surgeries.

My father was a jack of many trades. He worked as a barber, construction truck driver, meat cutter, delivery truck driver, cook, and restaurant manager. He persevered in the work force well into the 1970s when his back no longer accommodated physical labor.

I believe my tenacity, "empirical-mindedness," and, to some extent, anger come mainly from my father. My intelligence and ability to combine both "softness" and "hardness" come from both my parents.

I have much clearer memories of our second stay in Astoria (1955–1957). For example, I vividly remember disobeying my parents and climbing over a back fence to run in a field behind our apartment building. As I recall, they caught me doing this only once. I'd lingered too long on a pile of wood and sundry junk upon which I enjoyed climbing. It was probably more dangerous than I realized, but lots of fun. I never saw the rats that must have resided among the debris. My dad came home from work earlier than usual one day, parked his pickup truck in its customary spot in front of the building, and, before I knew it, appeared on the back steps. "Get in here," he barked. He watched me climb over the fence, reversing my

Odyssean course. "Don't do that again." As he lightly spanked me and sent me to my room, I recall seeing a sly grin on his face.

My dad was proud as a peacock when I, his first son, was born. We still retain a photo of his ex-Marine buddy, Danny, holding me. Because I sensed it would cause him pain, I never asked him if he was disappointed when he learned I would probably never be a Marine. He must have experienced enormous ambivalence. His subsequent actions spoke volumes. He seems to have sublimated feelings about my apparent incapacities, translating them into aspirations of my earning a PhD or becoming a lawyer. "You'll never succeed unless you get an education," became his mantra.

In those early days, I believe my father was secretly happy his son with bad eyes demonstrated a sense of adventure. He would forever wrestle with the conflict of wanting his firstborn son to be a "chip off the old block"— a rough-and-tumble city kid, a sandlot baseball player, a Marine. The realization that I had to be careful, move more slowly than other children my age, and take my lumps—painful as that might be for a parent to watch—steeled him against the sense of loss I know he felt. It also made him harsher than he may have wanted to be, demanding more of me, yet holding me back when my adventurous impulses began to mirror his own. Nonetheless, I would spend many hours in my youth playing in dangerous places, bumping into things and breaking eyeglass frames, and causing my parents, no doubt, hours of anxiety.

Spectacles

Eyeglasses became the bane of my young existence. One day, at about three and a half years old, I recall seeing a photo of myself a year younger. A handsome face stared back at me, untarnished by the spectacles that now "blemished" my physiognomy. In my heart, I somehow realized I had been injured by something I did not yet understand. As I cried and attempted to remove my glasses, my parents intervened, telling me I must wear them. Life, to my young mind, had become a monumental pain.

Luckily, eyeglasses corrected my vision to 20/70, which enabled me to read books and newspapers until late adolescence. I couldn't see in dark or dimly lit places or when I walked from bright sunlight (which hurt my eyes) into the relative darkness of a shadow or the inside of a building. Movie theaters proved impossible. Since all I could see was straight ahead, I constantly bumped into things just to the right and left of me. Since I tended to walk with my head down, in order to better see the ground, I often banged into low-hanging objects such as tree branches. My signature solution was a baseball cap with a brim pulled low to protect my head and shield my eyes from glare. Today, several scars mark my forehead, the result of multiple bouts of bumping my head into tree branches, bent-over signposts, and, once, a pipe with which a young playmate bopped me.

I can't even begin to estimate how many pairs of eyeglasses I broke running around, engaging in the wild play of childhood. If not for Dr. Paley, an understanding optometrist, I probably would have driven my already financially strapped family into bankruptcy. I banged my glasses so often the impact on the sides of my nose once resulted in a rash. I actually grew allergic to my glasses. My parents grew wise, procuring small rubber pads to stick on the nosepieces. These pads eased the trauma when I collided with external objects.

Life Changes

In 1957, my middle brother, Lenny, was born. I had thoroughly enjoyed the role of only child for the few years it lasted. Life changed forever with the birth of my first sibling. I most assuredly resented the loss of my regal status. It had comfortably allowed me to receive all the attention I wanted, and my world was under control. From my toddler's-eye view, the presence of another being in our household created chaos.

Although I don't recall the deed, my parents surmised I might be making a statement when, one day, to help my mom freshen him up, I emptied an entire bottle of baby powder on Lenny. A dozen years later, Lenny would get very sick and nearly die. I would come to cherish him with a fervor I couldn't imagine. The event would change me too.

Our migrations continued. Shortly after Lenny's birth, we moved again to Rockland County, this time settling in the neighboring village of West Haverstraw. We lived there until I left home to attend college fourteen years later.

The doctors told my parents that my condition would probably not appear in future offspring. Assured there was no need for them to worry about having additional children, they planned the rest of their family. This advice turned out to be wrong.

Although the doctors knew RP was a genetically induced condition, since no one in my extended family and no ancestors as far back as the turn of the twentieth century were known to have had a serious eye problem, it seemed that my situation was a random expression of a damaged gene. In their defense, in the mid-1950s, little was known about the genetics of RP. Since neither my cousins nor Lenny showed signs of RP, my condition appeared truly anomalous. In fact, today, two generations later, none of my cousins' children and grandchildren shows signs of the condition.

Two years later, in 1959, my youngest brother, Joseph, was born. On the alert for the condition, the doctors examined Joseph well before his first birthday. It didn't take them long to diagnose him with the same condition I had. Actually, his was worse. In addition to a degenerated retina, Joseph has nystagmus, an uncontrolled movement of the eyes that makes it impossible for him to read. He became a braille reader at age five and, as an adult, reads quite swiftly. I believe his inability to read print impeded his overall education. A smart guy, he had tremendous difficulty learning math and science—and he has a good head for both subjects.

"Down the Bank"

The 1950s witnessed the construction of housing developments by builders who erected block upon block of cookie-cutter homes the way farmers plant seeds. West Haverstraw was no exception. Except for different choices of color and styles of lawn manicuring, all the houses in our neighborhood looked quite similar. In 1957, my parents rented a one-floor A-frame house (no basement and a crawl-in attic) on Cameron Street, a side street three blocks from Railroad Avenue, the main street in town. By small-kid standards, we lived deep inside the development; by parental standards, it was a safe place for kids to play.

The neighborhood was ideal for the plethora of young children growing up there. Traffic on the streets was very light, and we could ride our bikes and play ball on them to our hearts' content. Bordering the development on its east side were the woods. Further to the east—about two miles away—loomed the Hudson River.

The entire area was historic. Battles and other incidents relating to the American Revolution (including the Battle of Stony Point, won by General Mad Anthony Wayne) took place near there. The site where Benedict Arnold handed Major John Andre the plans to West Point is also nearby.

The neighborhood in which we lived lay far uphill from the river, and peeking through the trees or down one of the side streets, you could always catch a glimpse of the river and, across the other side, the land rising up on the banks of Westchester County. For most of my life, I have lived within sight of the Hudson, a magnificent natural treasure. I have had the pleasure of boating upon it, swimming in it, diving beneath its surface, and simply regarding it as a symbol of my childhood stability.

The woods commenced at the edge of each property unfortunate enough to have been placed at the east side of the development. Kids were forced to trespass onto these properties to enter the woods. Although not expressly forbidden to go there, parents warned their children to be careful if they decided to enter the woods for a great game of army or to fish in the "big pond" located on the other side of the primeval expanse. "Little kids," as we preadolescents were called, were warned to watch out for snakes.

I didn't fully believe there actually were snakes in the woods until one day when a "big kid" captured a long snake, killed it, and then proceeded to parade it, hanging from a stick, around his block. I can still see it, vividly embedded in visual memory, hanging there.

The snake appeared to be at least three feet long. Terrified and growing queasy, I ran home to the safety of my mother's arms. The image gave me nightmares for years to come. Today, I retain a strong visceral fear of snakes—a primal instinct no doubt exacerbated by my inability to see.

In real life, I simply stay out of their habitat at all costs. Once, for example, it took me twenty-four hours to work up the nerve to leave a bungalow at a New Mexico resort because I didn't want to risk an encounter with one of the dozens of varieties of rattlesnakes (including the diamondback) boasted about in New Mexico travel literature. They should take more care with their advertising campaign.

Back in my old neighborhood, upon entering the woods, one experiences the ground dropping downhill rapidly, making for some great sleigh-riding in winter. Lenny and I spent many hours seeing how close we could get to near missing, with our sleds, the "big tree" at the bottom of the steepest hill. Because of this rapid shift in altitude, the geologists called the woods an embankment—we called them "the bank."

"Where are you going?" we'd ask each other.

"Down the bank," came the reply.

At age six, while playing with other children in one of the yards bordering the bank, an older boy, Frankie, asked me if I wanted to go on a hike into the woods. I clearly recall Lenny, a toddler of three and a half years, warning me not to go. Heeding him not, I marched with Frankie down the hills and into the trees.

We walked down, around several looping paths, through the cattails, beyond the last sleigh-riding path, and into the unknown. The Hudson River stood majestically in front of us to the east, but although I thought it should have been growing bigger (it seemed we'd been walking toward the river forever), its profile didn't change. Getting anxious, I asked Frankie to take me back. "Just go to the top of that hill," he pointed, "and call for your brother. He'll hear you and guide you home."

I did as I was told. I walked to the top of the hill and called. To my consternation, Lenny did not answer. I realized that the hills, trees, and underbrush all looked the same to me. I thought, "I have no idea where to go." Spinning around, I saw to my horror that Frankie had left me. I was alone.

Resolving not to die in the forest, I turned my back on the Hudson and began walking uphill. This was the only thing that made sense. After all, I reasoned through quakes of panic, we'd walked down hill to get here; uphill must be the way back to the yard, and Lenny, and home.

I walked as straight up the hills as I could, the fact that we had traveled a meandering course to the point of my undoing nagging at me all the while. "How can walking straight get me home when I know we made several turns?" I moaned aloud. Desperate and crying, I kept turning around to assure myself the river still lay behind me and repeatedly called for Lenny. When still he did not answer, I reverted to calling for my mother. She didn't answer either.

In retrospect, I probably walked for no more than thirty minutes, but it seemed like hours to my six-year-old and addled mind. Still, I managed to pull myself together enough to talk myself into believing I would get out of the woods sooner or later. Noticing an unmistakable hint of fading daylight, I burst into a fresh set of tears. I couldn't see in the dark. My time was limited.

Although at age six I didn't fully comprehend the ramifications of lack of peripheral vision, when I walked, I instinctively looked down at the ground, occasionally scanning from side to side to prevent tripping on ruts or objects immediately in my path or slightly to either side.

I'd forgotten to raise my eyes to scan my surroundings for quite a while. Then a miracle happened. I looked up and saw above me the most beautiful sight I'd ever seen. Atop the hill I'd been climbing, hovering silhouetted against the dusky sky like an angel, stood the symbol of my salvation: a trash can.

Scrambling up the hill and lunging toward the can, I prayed amid sobs that there would be a house or some representation of the human race connected to that can. God must have heard me, for I emerged at the edge of someone's backyard.

"Hello," I shouted at the top of my voice. I could see lights on inside the back window, but couldn't see well enough to know if anyone was actually home. I held my breath, releasing it only when I saw an older man and woman emerge from the back door and move slowly toward me.

The man called to me, "What can I do for you, young man?" His voice was kind. An even kinder voice emanated from the woman accompanying him. "He's crying. Bring him into the house."

Lifting me over a low fence, the elderly coupled hugged me and led me to their back door. A minute earlier, I was alone in the woods. Now, I found myself gratefully sitting in a nice warm kitchen.

"What's your name?"

"Anthony," I answered.

"Do you know your phone number?" Luckily, I did. They called my mother, told her I was all right, and asked her to "come take your little boy home."

Meanwhile, Lenny had completed his play and gone home. After careful questioning, my mother ascertained that her oldest son had gone into the woods with another boy. She began to worry. A half hour later, just as she was about to commence a search of the neighborhood, the phone rang.

Quickly turning off the stove and bundling up my newborn brother Joseph, she sprinted out of the house, forgetting to lock the front door. Carrying her infant in her arms and with Lenny running alongside her, my mother traversed the six-block equivalent space between our house and that of my rescuers in about ten minutes. By the time she got there, I had downed several cookies and a delicious glass of milk and had quite nicely, thank you, recovered from my ordeal. I'm not sure my mother has yet. These many decades later, she continues to scold me for "going into those woods like that."

Perhaps I too haven't fully recovered. To this day, I still shiver a little when I recall the details of my adventure. Trash cans retain a special place in my heart, and my love of cookies has not diminished. Probably most important, I still look, both literally and figuratively, with trepidation upon the uncertainties of uncharted terrain. I feel more comfortable, for example, with a plan of action, a sense of how things work, and an understanding of what is normally expected in social situations.

I did learn one lesson: to trust Lenny's judgment when it comes to right and wrong. He became my moral barometer. While growing up, whenever I thought about pulling a prank or venturing beyond the bounds of parental permission, I looked to Lenny for his opinion. If he said okay, we went for it. If he said no, I usually didn't risk breaking a rule I well knew I shouldn't.

Problematic was the fact that Lenny wasn't always consistent. Years later, for example, while at play, Lenny and I were attacked by neighborhood kids in a field that contained piles of dirt and stones. A rock-throwing fight ensued with Lenny and I pinned behind one pile of dirt and the "enemy" behind another. Lenny drew first blood, nailing one of the neighborhood kids on the head. In the meeting that followed, my parents learned that he had suffered a small cut and mild bump and would be just fine. Unfortunately, the worm turned on me.

As I opened my mouth to defend Lenny, the neighbor kid's older sister, there to defend her brother and get revenge, proceeded to tell my father that I had recently sassed the school bus driver. Lenny remained silent. It was I who ended up on the receiving end of a mighty spanking for being disrespectful to my elders. Somehow, Lenny managed to go unscathed.

Public School or Bust

My parents' decision to return to Astoria in 1955 rotated on my future education, a major concern for them. Despite having obtained little formal education themselves, they both valued education highly. My father who had dropped out of high school and joined the Marine Corps at age seventeen, eventually earned a high school equivalency diploma while in hospital twenty years later. My mother, growing up in Sicily during World War II, had her education terminated in the fifth grade. Enrolling in public school as a new immigrant and with a paucity of English language skills, she quickly encountered taunts and teasing from American children. Realizing that school was not for her, she went to work in a factory as soon as she turned sixteen.

In 1958, having moved back to the suburbs, my parents were confronted with an offer they steadfastly refused. School officials, having no experience with visually impaired children, told them to send me to Lavelle, a Catholic residential school for the blind in the Bronx. My parents, believing that I would become institutionalized if I went there, and not wishing to have me live away from them, declined. Instead, they insisted on enrolling me in the local public elementary school.

My father knew about sight conservation teachers whose special training made them knowledgeable in how to teach blind or partially sighted children. They were called "sight conservation" teachers because it was thought that if visually impaired children refrained as much as possible from using their eyes, their small amount of remaining vision would be prolonged. In those days, some of the residential schools for the blind took this to the extreme, teaching children with good reading vision to read only in braille. Today, the pendulum has swung in the opposite direction. The special teachers are now called teachers of visually impaired students (TVIs), and many children who rightfully should use braille because their reading is slow and labored when they use their eyes are not being taught braille early enough.

Since a TVI had become available to visit me in school and supplement the efforts of my classroom teachers, the district agreed to my parents' demand that I be placed in public school. I did well, academically. I could read my textbooks, albeit more slowly than my classmates. I even won reading awards in the early grades. I could see the blackboard so long as I sat front and center.

Mrs. Crawford, my "special teacher," came once a week and pulled me from class. She taught me how to take notes in a nifty shorthand that involved omitting all vowels. She taught me a word game that I still play today. It involves making as many words from the letters of a very long word as you can. Most important, Mrs. Crawford made sure I could do my homework and master everything academic.

Two things I didn't master included avoidance of playground injuries and the constant taunts ("four-eyes," "Mr. Magoo," "How many fingers do I have up?") of the other children. The scars from the taunting are perhaps just as visible in my personality today as those that show on my forehead. I became an early nerd. The girls didn't take me seriously. I was last to be picked for playground teams. Still I tried, albeit with less-than-stellar acumen, to play with the others at school and in the neighborhood.

A close call when I was twelve years old should have awakened us to the need for me to learn braille. Just prior to entering junior high school, when, among other things, students were required to change classes for the first time in their lives, I lost most of the vision in my right eye. All I could see out of the eye was blur. Worse yet, the failing right eye threw images on what I could see with my left eye. I had difficulty reading, was unable to see the lines on regular paper, and couldn't seem to learn my way around my new school. Unable to do my homework the first night of school, I crawled into bed and began to cry. My mother comforted me while my father, always one step ahead, brought some bold-lined paper to my room. "Try this," he encouraged. It worked; I could write without drifting in a downward slant.

Junior high school officials assigned a classmate to escort me from class to class, permitting me to leave a minute before the change bell. A new itinerant TVI, Mrs. Maglin, procured large-print books for me. Mrs. M. had worked with my youngest brother, Joseph, for a few years and was more than happy to assist me. She taught me about bold-lined paper and dark-inked pens, instructed me to sit front and center in all my classes, and provided tips on how to constructively get help from students and teachers. I had to act in ways I never had to before, all the while sensing that my schoolmates regarded me as different.

Years later, I learned that the school nurse, preceding me into homeroom on the first day, might have exacerbated the taunting I would continue to experience. She told the class that a visually impaired boy would be joining them and they were to treat me just like everyone else. "You never had a chance," a friend related over dinner fifteen years later. "Once the nurse told us about you, we just had to find ways to tease you."

"Adults don't always know what is best for children," I muttered, realizing that years of grief might have been worsened by a well-meaning act of a school official.

We visited Dr. Bonocolto to see if he could do anything about the loss of vision in my right eye. He examined me and said, "I think it's a problem with the circulation." He gave me a shot and sent us back to West Haverstraw. A few weeks later, to my great joy and relief, the vision in my right eye cleared. I gave up the bold-lined paper and, by the following year, the large-print books, but retained the practice of sitting front and center in all my classes. Life returned to normal.

In the ensuing years, the vision in my right eye deteriorated more quickly than the vision in my left, disappearing forever in my early thirties. In the meantime, I had dodged a bullet I was not yet emotionally ready to absorb.

Young Jock

I was less than a stellar athlete as a child. My pitching arm was wild, I ran slower than the proverbial tortoise, and my prowess in the push-up and chin-up competitions in gym class was, at best, average. For some reason, perhaps because my stomach got a lot of exercise digesting Mom's delicious cooking, I managed to do well in sit-up contests. Thankfully, with practice, I was able to develop good agility. This, in concert with a decent sense of balance, enabled me to avoid many injuries I might otherwise have incurred. Given I was always tripping over something, it helped that I could quickly regain my body orientation and land on my feet instead of my face.

My biggest disappointment was my inability to play baseball. Because I couldn't see a hardball in flight, my relationship to the game was relegated to watching the Yankees on television or sneaking a portable radio into bed to listen to late-night cliff-hangers.

"Do you think Anthony would be a good player?" my mother asked my father. "He loves the game so much."

It was a hot August night in 1964. Mel Stottlemyre had just won another game en route to saving the Yankees' season and leading them to yet another World Series. My parents sat in the living room watching the Little League baseball World Series on TV.

"He would be good in that he'd play hard," he answered. I crawled out from the covers, reversed my position on the bed, and craned my neck to hear more.

"I was going to get him a glove, but I'm afraid we'd just be encouraging him too much," my father continued. "He can't see the ball, and he's always breaking his glasses. We can't afford it." I stopped listening. Devastated, I turned back to my pillow, buried my head, and cried.

In my anguish, I realized a deeper powerlessness than most children should have to experience. Something I loved more than anything was out of reach, no matter how hard I might try. The tears flowed, and I seethed with anger. This wasn't the first time I'd felt powerlessness due to my visual impairment. Remembering only a few years prior when I tried to reject wearing eyeglasses, I thought, "I knew right from the start this would be bad." I've occasionally wondered over the years if this was the genesis of my seeking compensation, not so much for visual impairment, but perhaps for the loss of power to obtain things or activities that would make me happy.

Softball was a bit different. With a sufficiently white ball and dark background behind the batter or thrower, I could visually track a softball from as far away as one hundred feet or so. This meant the kids could put me in the outfield, safely away from infield hot spots, and hope I would stay out of the way. They knew I was a decent thrower once I chased down a ball, so perhaps they hoped I would get the ball to the infield before the batter rounded the bases.

My problems on the field were compounded by reduced opportunity to practice and improve my skills. As is usually the case, the better players got more playing time, the lesser ones sat on the bench. Thus with precious few opportunities to excel, I was convinced that there was no way I could ever be competitive in sports. My reputation as a poor hitter and fielder cemented itself in the kid-lore of my neighborhood and playground. Many had witnessed my tracking a ball all the way into my glove, only to drop it. They'd seen me strike out so often that when I made contact, the news spread, mockingly, throughout the neighborhood. When it came time to select players for a pickup game, they did everything they could to avoid having me on their teams. Only the intervention of teachers and the occasional peer defender ensured I would get a few at bats.

One good thing happened. I became known as a power hitter. In my anxiety to do well and, perhaps, in the anger I felt knowing I would more likely strike out than make contact, I swung hard at everything pitched to me. Thus I would, on rare occasions, whack one over the heads of unaware infielders, skipping it between surprised outfielders all the way to the fence. The opposition adjusted.

"Stay back," the defense would call. "He'll probably strike out, but if he hits it, it'll go far."

These rare occasions taught me something about what it feels like to have power. In the swing of a bat, I was transformed from Clark Kent to Superman, from the butt of jokes to someone awesome. I loved it. What's more, these events—rare indeed—elevated, albeit temporarily, my reputation and self-respect. For those few moments while the kids applauded and slapped my back as I crossed home plate, I felt powerful.

By midadolescence, I'd developed enough arm strength to throw a mean football. My natural throwing mechanics matched perfectly with the motion one uses to hurl a pigskin. I could cock the ball behind my right ear and, if necessary, deliver it wherever I wanted to with little more than a quick flick of my wrist or a strong thrust of my forearm. Admittedly, even if I'd had sufficient eyesight to join the football team—which clearly I didn't—I wouldn't have matched up against "real" quarterbacks who could toss the ball much farther than the forty yards I could master at my burliest. Nonetheless, I was able to loft long spirals and throw twenty-yard bullets, qualifying me as a pretty good playground helmsman.

My athletic shortcomings can only be partially explained by dearth of talent. Some credit can legitimately be assigned to poor eyesight. Beyond the already-mentioned impediments on the baseball field, lack of peripheral vision made it nearly impossible to follow a basketball in close quarters. Competitors easily stole the ball from me when I dribbled, and my judgment of the distance and location of the hoop was often inaccurate. In those days, we did not think about adapting the game by, for example, placing a sound projecting device behind the back board or using a beep basketball.

I could also toss a mean dodgeball. This was a particularly frightening game. Each side contained so many boys one could barely move on the court, no less elude an oncoming projectile. I hung in there until the gym teacher made the situation impossible for me by introducing a second ball into the game. There was no way I could keep my eye on both balls. In that event, I resorted to hiding behind teammates. I even hid behind bleachers that stood folded against the back walls of the gym. The sound of balls smashing into them made it seem like an artillery barrage. Cringing and gritting my teeth, I would wait until I sensed a thinning of the ranks on the floor. My purpose in hiding was to avoid being hit in the face until there was enough space for me to keep my eye on both balls. Then I would emerge. Since I could throw hard and catch the large kickballs we used, I was well able to compete against even the meanest and hardest throwing opponents.

Football presented daunting challenges. On the field, it was impossible for me to see would-be tacklers coming at me from the side. In neighborhood games, quick and agile runners easily darted around me. I ran tentatively, never knowing if an obstacle lay just to my left or right. I had difficulty seeing through the face guard of the football helmet, and guards worn over my eyeglasses distorted my vision and made me feel claustrophobic. Playing without glasses, the solution most often suggested by the coaches, detracted from my vision so much I couldn't see the ball in flight, something I could do with my glasses on. So long as the distance from the thrower was not far and there weren't too many players on the field keeping me from spotting the ball as it left the quarterback's hand, I made a creditable pass receiver. The minute things got cluttered out there, my performance diminished. Nevertheless, I ached to join the high school football team.

One autumn day in my fifteenth year, I attended a preseason orientation meeting. I sat in the cafeteria surrounded by boys much bigger and heavier than me and listened with growing consternation as the football coach described the practice routine, positions for which we could try out, and the size and strength requirements for each spot on the team. I thought, "What the heck am I doing here?" My answer: "Because you love football" and "What a great way to get into shape."

The moment of truth came when it was time to fill out the application form. The lightness of the print on the page and the rough-and-tumble atmosphere in the room combined to turn the tide. I was much too embarrassed to ask for help filling out the form.

If I needed that much help right from the start, how could I possibly survive on the gridiron?

"This is insane," I thought. "There's no way you can see well enough to do this. You'll get killed out there."

Rising slowly, I sneaked out of the room, hoping no one would see me. If anyone asked, I thought I would say I was there more out of curiosity than serious intent. I didn't want it to be known that I had tried to act out a fantasy. No one asked. In fact, they didn't seem to notice me at all.

My head pounded with a mixture of emotions. On one hand, I breathed a sigh of relief to be out of the insane situation in which I had just placed myself. On the other hand, I mourned the loss of a fantasy. As if this wasn't painful enough, the loss of a way to get into better shape left me with the problem I had hoped to solve when I entered the room. After all, I mused, it's hard to drive yourself as hard as a coach can drive you. Football would have helped me develop strength and stamina. Not only that, I would not be able to accrue some of the adulation meted out to members of the football team—especially by the cheerleaders. I would have to find another way to improve my physical, not to mention my social, stature. Luckily, a few years prior, I had discovered wrestling—something I could compete in at a formal team level.

To the Mat

The scene: Fifth-grade gym class. Our teacher, Mr. Mercurio, spread mats on the floor, divided us into two groups, and told us a little about a sport called wrestling. He said that combatants meet in the center of the mat, circle, and lunge at each other in an attempt to get a thing called a "takedown." He described the object of the game: "to pin your opponent's shoulders to the mat for two whole seconds."

We sat around a cushioned mat containing an inner or center circle and an outer boundary circle. Mr. Mercurio explained that wrestlers commence action in the center circle and must remain within the total confines of the outer circle (about thirty-two feet in diameter) throughout the match. If they go out of bounds, the referee stops action and returns the grapplers to the center circle.

Mr. Mercurio was a man of few words. Without further instruction, he paired me with Paul, a heavyset boy whom I'd always feared on the playground. Paul was bigger than me and much stronger. How could our teacher think this was a fair matchup? Perhaps because neither of us knew what we were doing!

Following orders, we walked to the center of the mat, faced off, and waited for something to happen. Fearing that if I locked arms with him, I would certainly be outmuscled, I concentrated on staying clear of Paul's grasp. As we circled and stalked each other, Paul's face was fixed in a permanent growl. His biceps rippled. His hands threatened to twist me into a pretzel. I noticed his legs were totally exposed. A plan coalesced in my brain.

Continuing to circle and inching closer, crouching and catlike, I waited for my opportunity. It came in a flash. Allowing my body to take control and forsaking all care, I half squatted, reached behind Paul's thighs, grabbed them, and pulled hard.

My dismal athletic history, short as it was and not one of a playground fighter, caused me to predict that my strength would be insufficient to budge Paul's legs. In that case, I surmised, he would pick me up and slam me to the mat. My career as a wrestler and possibly my life would end then and there.

Fortunately, my plan didn't crash. In fact, my aspirations, not to mention my body, didn't meet with any harm at all. Instead, Paul's legs went out from under him and, as I had imagined might happen, he fell flat on his back. Diving on top of him, I applied pressure upon his shoulders with all my strength. The only sounds I heard were Paul's breathing in one ear and the shouts of my classmates in the other. Holding my breath and bearing down, I heard the sound that gave me the biggest thrill of my young life and the one that launched my athletic career: the simultaneous shrill of my gym teacher's whistle and the slap of his hand upon the mat. He called out loud and clear, "Pin!"

A surge of relief coursed through me. Until that moment, I had truly believed it was my destiny to be forever trounced. Instead, I felt powerful. Not only had Paul failed to wipe the mat with me, I had taken him down. I'd also erased the growl from his face. From that time on, he didn't bully me on the playground. In fact, he treated me with kindness.

The feeling of power was wonderful, but it did not come without emotional dissonance. Nearly subliminal at the time, I would not have known the cause. Amplified now by years of reflection, I now understand that I was experiencing a feeling of energy loss. The feeling was not unlike what I felt in situations when I didn't understand a class lesson: sad and drained. It was the same feeling I felt when striking out in a softball game. My head would droop, and the wind would pass out of my sails. This time was different. The feeling was there in the midst of victory.

At that time, I was capable of only partially crystalizing the reason. A memory, the photo, the one of me at age two without eyeglasses, reemerged into consciousness. I had an inkling that something psychically "bad" might have happened to me back then. What was it? What about the memory of that photo could explain this energy drain?

Standing on the mat in gym class, savoring my first win as a grappler, I began to comprehend. Wearing glasses had changed the way I looked, but more important was what it represented: diminished mastery of the world around me. Adding insult to injury was the fact my eyesight was still poor despite my wearing them! Thus began the process of understanding that my life would consist of a never-ending battle between ability and disability.

Wrestling turned out to be the only sport where I have naturally excelled. It felt intuitive. Moves came to me much as an artist conceptualizes a painting or an architect a building. I ad-libbed as I went along. Everything I attempted seemed to work. I pinned all my opponents.

In elementary school, no one could beat me, except Joey.

I barely held my own against him. When we faced off in the elementary school championship, each of us having defeated two others to get there, we were regarded as being evenly matched. We rolled around, grunted and groaned, and did very little else. It took all of our respective strength to keep each of us from pinning the other. In the final analysis, I believe Joey wrestled better. Technically, he would have won on points, but at this early stage of our career, the coach wasn't counting. Because I grew taller and heavier than him, this was the last time Joey and I would compete. Crowned as co-champions, we went off to junior high school convinced we were good.

Junior high school wrestling was uneventful, except that I learned my trade, so to speak. I learned that the wrestling contest between two teams is called a "meet"; the contest between two individuals is called a "match." Matches are divided into three periods, each two minutes in length. College and Olympic matches may last longer.

I met my first "real" official in junior high school wrestling. Aided by a scorekeeper/clock manager who sits at a table to the side of the mat, the referee awards points as contestants successfully complete their maneuvers. He is there to keep the wrestlers from hurting each other, especially by stopping action if either wrestler uses an illegal move such as a slam or pushing against a joint's normal way of bending. This is the opposite of the martial arts where leveraging an arm by pushing the elbow against itself is how one gets an opponent to move in a desired direction. Years later when I took a basic judo class, I felt so squeamish about pushing against joints, it inhibited my performance.

The young men with whom I wrestled were all committed to the sport and, on average, much better than the unwilling amateurs I conquered in elementary school. We learned how to work out. The coaches taught us exercises specific to wrestling—the bridge (to build strong neck muscles), the spin (to build speed and agility in moving from in front of an opponent to behind him), power push-ups, stand-ups, sit-outs, rolls, tumbles, twists and turns we'd never done before. It was exhausting.

A few months after the conclusion of the seventh grade season, I managed to break my right arm in a neighborhood ball game. Junior high school classes took place in the Haverstraw High School building, requiring split shifts with high school classes scheduled in the morning and junior high in the afternoons. I used the mornings to do homework, play alone for a few minutes in the yard, and devour Mom's delicious lunches. This schedule and the relative inactivity pressed upon me after breaking my arm combined to cause me to gain weight. In fact, I grew fat. Consequently, in eighth grade, I found myself pitted against larger and stronger opponents who easily overpowered me. This persisted into the next season and was so demoralizing that halfway through, I quit, thinking I would never return to wrestling. That year, Joey became a county champion.

The summer after my freshman year, I attended a five-week camp for blind children in Batavia, a small town halfway between Rochester and Buffalo in northwestern New York State. The summer program was set up by a school for the blind to teach us how to get along using limited eyesight or none at all. We learned how to do our laundry, cook, clean, properly groom ourselves, travel with a cane, and more. It was my first experience under sleep shades (blindfolds). I didn't like it, but I knew learning to function nonvisually would be a key to success in dark conditions and (perish the thought from my young mind) should I ever lose all my remaining vision.

The gym coach was a visually impaired slave driver who got us into shape. One day, I challenged him to a wrestling match. In wrestling terms, he tied me up in knots. I couldn't do much more than grovel on my belly for the entire grapple. Livid with myself for being so slow and weak, I questioned whether I had what it took to be a good wrestler. Why did I feel so powerless? The coach admonished, "You've got to get tougher and move faster." My father's voice reverberated from head to toe: "He'd be good in that he would play hard," I recalled him saying. Why, I asked myself, did it seem that I wasn't wrestling as hard as I could? Was there something different about wrestling than, say, softball or football, which I played hard all the time? Might the intimacy of the grapple be psychologically close to the corporal punishment and verbal criticism my father meted out? I am sure this thought did not reach consciousness. The conflict unprocessed, I vowed to try harder.

That summer, I improved my conditioning and lost weight. That is also when I learned to run. The coach showed us how to use guide rails that helped us safely run one-hundred-yard dashes at a full sprint. The rails enabled us to run in a straight line while holding a ring that encircled a long guy-wire. Those of us with some vision also ran unguided on the circular cinder track.

By the end of eight weeks, I was able to run the mile in six minutes, twenty seconds. In all the running I did as an adult, I never got much faster than that. The revelation that it was possible for me to run more than the short sprints and one-hundred-yard dashes I'd been accustomed to running as a child meant I could use distance running to develop stamina. Stamina, as I would learn again and again, would be a key to success in wrestling.

The coach taught us how to do pull-ups, throw a medicine ball, and lift weights. I noticed my adolescent body beginning to change. In two critical months late in my fourteenth year, I managed to transform myself from an endomorph to a mesomorph—from a near-roly-poly boy to a solidly built adolescent. By the time the tenth grade wrestling season came around, and recovered from my aborted attempt to join the football team, I had developed a true wrestling physique, replete with bulging biceps, protruding pectorals, a six-pack stomach, and more. I returned to the mats with renewed vigor.

Grappling

> Two bronzes, but they were passing bronze before
> The sculptor
> All glint, all gleaming, face to face and grace
> To grace
> Balanced almost beyond their balance, tingling
> To spring—
> Who ever saw so point-by-point, so perfect
> A pair
> That either one—or both—or neither one—
> Could win… ("Two Wrestlers" by Robert Francis)

Wrestling is considered by many to be the oldest sport on earth. Pictorial representations of grappling survive from ancient Egypt, Greece, and Rome. In fact, many of the holds used today can be seen in prehistoric cave paintings. The first recorded Olympic wrestling match occurred in the games of 708 BC. Highly valued as a form of military exercise without weapons, wrestling quickly evolved into two forms. Orthia pale (upright and proper wrestling) required opponents to throw each other to the ground. Three falls constituted a loss. Kato pale (ground wrestling) required one opponent to signal defeat by raising his right hand with the index finger pointed.

Today, most Americans know about two major types of amateur wrestling, Greco-Roman and freestyle. Greco-Roman wrestling is the modern version of orthia pale, with emphasis placed on wrestling in the standing position and tilting the back toward the mat, away from a ninety-degree angle. This is called "exposing" the back. Freestyle wrestling most resembles the type of wrestling done in high school and college. It is the modern version of kato pale, emphasizing action down on the mats. A healthy infusion of upright or standing wrestling makes freestyle an eclectic form of wrestling. Other names include *catch-as-catch-can*, *scholastic*, and *collegiate*.

Wrestlers compete in discreet weight classes. These differ between high school (somewhat smaller and lighter contestants) and the college and freestyle arenas. Wrestlers weigh in before the start of a match. The attending referee qualifies each contestant for the weight class to which they belong. In New York high schools, the lightest weight class is 98 pounds, and the heaviest weight class is the 285 pound class. I wrestled in the 138-pound class in high school and the 167-pound class in college.

Among the anxiety-provoking elements endemic to wrestling competition is the relative inactivity of waiting for your turn to go out on the mats. Competitors who wrestle in the middleweight classes must sit through several matches, cheering on their comrades, before it is their turn. Pity the heavyweights who wrestle last. Today, coaches and officials can agree to a random drawing to determine which weight class will begin the match. All subsequent matches follow the weight class sequence. I am happy to see this rule on the books. By time it was my turn to wrestle, I was often emotionally drained. If I'd been able to wrestle first, I would have done so with my energy reserves more intact.

It was my sophomore year in high school. We sat in a circle on the wall-to-wall mat in the wrestling room. The temperature has been raised to ninety degrees to help us avoid muscle pulls. Coach Daniels had already evaluated the enormous talent he'd just inherited from the junior high school team.

"The sophomore group is the most talented we've received in a long time. Jake, Joe, Anthony, David, Ken, Teddy, and Tucker, I expect all of you to make the varsity along with Jim and Joey."

The way things lined up, it appeared I had a chance to make varsity at the 138- to 140-pound weight class. Jim, a fellow "smart class" student, had emerged from junior high school wrestling far more experienced and muscular than me. It turned out he, along with Joey, who I'd wrestled to a stalemate in elementary school and who had already proven himself a champion, had attended a summer wrestling camp while I was in Batavia. No one had approached me about the wrestling camp, or surely I would have gone.

A few juniors and seniors rounded out the lineup that year. David, a powerfully built guy and fellow sophomore who would eventually become the high school starting quarterback, beat me to make varsity. I would wrestle under Mr. McGuire as the junior varsity 138-pounder.

Coach Daniels continued. "I know you will attempt to lose as much weight as possible before wrestle-offs begin. I caution you not to try to lose weight in artificial ways. We all know what those are."

The group chuckled. The coach was referring to unorthodox dieting and use of other unhealthy methods to shed pounds. Instead, he offered, "If your parents can afford it, have a steak every night." I shuddered. There was no way my parents could afford that. "And when I refer to your bread and butter move," he quipped, "I don't mean at the dinner table."

Wrestlers generally shed pounds in order to qualify for weight classes below their off-season weight. Most of the weight loss is accomplished under controlled and safe conditions. For example, the rules dictate that wrestlers cannot lose more than a certain portion of their body weight from the point of the official preseason weigh-in. Body fat composition and hydration tests are also a part of the process that dictates the minimum weight class in which wrestlers will be able to compete.

The usual way of losing weight is to adjust one's diet, increasing protein intake, and reducing carbohydrate and fat consumption. This, in concert with heavy exercise and lots of sweating in the heated workout room, usually does the trick.

Unfortunately, a few wrestlers engaged in unauthorized and somewhat dangerous practices. I occasionally did. For example, when desperate, some of us resorted to extreme ways of sweating such as running in heavy sweat suits in hot places like the balcony over the school swimming pool. Others took laxatives to induce excretion. This at least permitted them to eat and then lose the weight right away. We knew for example that a glass of water can add a half pound; ten small Dixie cups of spit could get rid of it. These practices should be avoided; good diet and hard exercise work just fine.

High School Years

During the off-season prior to tenth grade and after returning home from Batavia, I lifted weights and ran. For fun, I played sandlot football with my friends (becoming a decent amateur quarterback) and, as I had done throughout my childhood, continued to romp the woods and factory grounds near my home. On many weekend days, I played and roughhoused from dawn until dusk.

During my sophomore and junior years, I wrestled on the junior varsity squads. I recall a match my sophomore year when I wrestled against a county champion. For some reason, he had been relegated to the junior varsity that day. Perhaps he had violated a school rule and this was his punishment; perhaps he failed to make weight in the next lower class. In any case, there I was, facing a big, strong, and extremely fast African American fellow.

The first period began with both of us standing at opposite sides of the center circle. This is the "neutral" position. The object was for one of us to take the other down to the mat. Once on the mat, which happened quickly, we were wrestling parterre. His ultimate objective was to pin me—that is, press both my shoulders to the mat for two seconds. If I could outlast his attempts to pin me, I figured I would still lose, but by points. At least, I thought dismally, the other team would earn fewer points than if he pinned me.

In the second period, we started parterre. Based on a coin toss, my opponent chose to begin the period in the top (advantage) position. I was in the bottom (disadvantage) position. Most grapplers select the top position for period two as it is easier to score points from the bottom position. Which is where you want to be in the third period if you are trailing in the match. In this match, there was no way my burly opponent was ever going to be in trouble. As it was, I spent the entire second period failing to escape and take down my opponent or pull a reversal of position to gain the advantage. These maneuvers would have scored me points. Instead, I grew exhausted and prayerful for my well-being.

In the third period, my opponent quickly escaped and took me down. It happened so fast I didn't have a chance to fight him off. Then he worked me into a pinning combination. These are maneuvers that render the unfortunate "victim" on his back. My favorite pinning combination (although I never got it to work in a competitive match) was the "double arm bar and figure four on the head." The move is now illegal, presumably due to the danger of wrapping legs around an opponent's neck.

My opponent used a simple "half nelson" to turn me over. When I fought back to my stomach, he used a more devastating pinning combination: the "cradle." This move pinches the head and knees together and makes it easy for the aggressive wrestler to turn his opponent onto his back and earn the pin. It worked as diagrammed, and my day was over.

I rationalized the experience as one of those occasions in my career when I was completely outclassed. If I could rewrestle the match, I certainly would stay away from a direct lockup to avoid those quick takedowns. In fact, the experience taught me how to size up an opponent in a split second, about all the time one really has if he is to recognize his opponent's strength and avoid getting mauled. Unfortunately, the experience also left me a bit traumatized.

STAND UP OR SIT OUT

My senior year began with a sit-in. Although we had just emerged from the 1960s, this form of protest was still in vogue. Somehow, I was the catalyst. It came to be known that in a preseason review, the school doctor had decided to bar me from wrestling. His inexplicable decision occurred just when I'd be most likely to make varsity.

Ignoring the years I had wrestled without injury, the doctor's explanation centered on a fear that my vision would be harmed by strenuous activity. Coach Daniels protested, and in what I speculate must have been either the final straw in arguments between him and the administration or his extreme sense of right and wrong, Mr. D. resigned his post. At least, those were the rumors, and they've never been disconfirmed.

Believing those rumors, the entire student body decided to rally behind this well-liked coach. Along with the wrestling team, the next morning, close to one thousand students sat on the floor of the school lobby to protest the wrongdoing and probably to be a part of school history. Ignoring a direct order from the principal, they refused to move. Realizing that at that moment the students were taking their cue from the wrestlers, the administration agreed to meet with the team if we told the students to return to class. We agreed.

As we strode into his office, the principal greeted us warmly, making a special point of saying hello to me. Not knowing why, I feared I was about to be suspended. We told him we wanted our coach back. In exchange for a promise of good behavior, he seemed to readily agree to see what he could do. Later, we suspected negotiations must have already gone on behind closed doors because after a few days, Coach D. was back in the gym. The wrestling team and the student body were happy.

My own situation dragged on a few weeks longer. Again, negotiations went on behind closed doors. One day, while sitting in the school cafeteria along with scores of other seniors taking the New York State Regents Scholarship exam, a woman tapped me on the shoulder and whispered, "It's okay, don't worry." I had no idea whom was speaking with or what she meant. I also didn't have time to ponder the issue. At that moment, I happened to be sitting alone at a table taking one of the more important examinations of my life. I was alone because my exam was provided to me in large font, and proctors thought it would be easy for others to see my answers if they sat too close. Winning a Regents Scholarship would mean that a large portion of my college tuition would be paid for. Fortunately, the interruption didn't affect my test performance. I won, not one, but two scholarships.

Later, I learned that while I was taking the test, several people, including my father, were meeting with the principal and the doctor to get me restored to the team. Incensed that I might be worried about my future wrestling career in the midst of taking an important exam, someone was dispatched to calm my nerves. It had almost done the opposite.

As I mentioned, I ended up winning two scholarships, one of which defrayed some of my college tuition. The other was a mistake. Somehow, probably by accidentally checking the wrong box on the cover sheet of my large print exam booklet, I managed to win a scholarship to nursing school. In those days, nursing was still the province of women. I learned about my accidental nursing scholarship in a most painful way.

One day, at the end of gym class, as I walked, naked, in the boy's locker room, returning from the shower, the announcement that I had won a free pass to nursing school came over the public address system. It took weeks for the welts imparted to my buttocks from dozens of towel snaps to heal and even longer before my friends stopped razzing me. I returned the scholarship, which I'm sure benefited someone else.

That year, I prepared for wrestling with more diligence than ever. Adhering to a strict weight-lifting schedule from the close of the previous season and practicing with the school swim team before the start of the new season helped get me into shape.

In my senior year, I wrestled part-time for both the junior and senior varsity squads, doing quite well for the former but only managing to win a few matches with the "big club." One match that I wrestled with the JV squad still makes me chuckle.

At that point in my physical development, not to mention the level to which my skills had evolved, it was clear that I should be competing at the varsity level. However, one day I found myself subbing on the JV squad for the regular 138-pound wrestler. My opponent, young and inexperienced, gaped at me during the weigh-in. He was short and a bit chunky; I was tall, V-shaped, and obviously much stronger than he.

The match lasted less than forty-five seconds. We circled each other in the neutral position. Guessing that my reflexes were faster and my strength greater than his, I allowed my opponent to make contact. Grabbing his arm, I spun him around and picked him up from behind, easing him to the mat; and before he could raise himself to his hands and knees, I ran a half nelson (a levering hold on the neck) and pried him onto his back. The pin call sounded not nearly as sweet as when I beat Paul in my first match in elementary school, but it sounded good nonetheless. The tables had certainly turned from two years prior when I had been "rooked" by that county champion. Afterward, the JV coach, Mr. McGuire, came up to me and said, "Thanks for the points." Being a hired gun sure felt nice.

That year, I sustained the only significant injury of my wrestling career. Jimmy, a junior and a star football player, had joined the wrestling team. Stocky and powerful, he easily made the varsity. On the football field, this 180-pound pure athlete became an all-American running back. He also doubled as a defensive back and the team's kicker.

I knew I shouldn't have done it. In a practice drill, I decided to intertwine my legs with Jimmy's, a hold designed to keep him from escaping my grasp. By the time I realized my foolishness, it was too late. With his tree trunk thighs, Jimmy's sudden "kick out" broke the hold and injured my right knee, robbing me forever of its full health. My teammates gathered around me as I yelped in pain. The worst of it lasted only a minute or two and then, strangely, subsided.

Although I continued wrestling that year as though nothing had happened, the incident weakened my knee in subtle ways. I noticed, for example, that I could no longer punt a football straight because my leg wobbled as it came forward during the kicking motion. Since

I had no plans to play football on any but the sandlot level, I thought little of it. I didn't experience the full manifestation of the knee injury until years later when, as an adult, I took up long-distance running.

Jimmy went on to play football at the University of Maryland, alongside the Dallas Cowboys Hall of Famer, Randy White. He finished his football career with a brief stint in the Canadian Football League. I believe he became a high school teacher. Years later, I would have occasion to meet Randy White, and we would reminisce about our mutual friend.

A key match, one I should have won, turned out to be critical to the varsity team's standing in the county that year. Wrestling in my usual 138-pound weight class, I found myself overmatched and trailing my opponent as the bout drew to a close. Worst of all, I had mentally sunk to the lowest level a wrestler can sink: feeling gratitude that I hadn't gotten pinned. This meant that the opposing team would receive only three points instead of six.

My nemesis attempted to put me into a cradle, a pinning combination from which it is virtually impossible to escape. In a desperate maneuver, I kicked free of the hold, rotated my body, and, to my surprise, landed atop my opponent's chest. Realizing he was on his back, I scrambled to apply pressure to his shoulders; but because I was in an awkward position, I was unable to hold them down long enough for the referee to call a pin. My opponent struggled to roll to his side. Since he still retained partial control of me, I had to desperately maneuver in order to prevent him from regaining the advantage and scoring more points. As I held on for dear life, I hoped the referee would award me points for the near-fall predicament (one or two shoulders down, but not long enough by rule for a pin to be called) in which I had just placed my adversary. The points were granted, but they were not enough for me to pull off a last-second victory.

Walking off the mat, I looked down so I wouldn't see the referee raise my opponent's hand over his head, the victory signal. My head was hung low also to avoid meeting the eyes of my teammates. I wanted to crawl into a cocoon; I'd let them down. Somehow, over the hometown cheers for my opponent, I was able to discern the voice of a single spectator loudly berating the referee. It was North Rockland's assistant football coach, Mr. Casarella, shouting, "He had him pinned! He had him pinned. That was a bum call, Ref!"

The castigation being of no avail, the call stood. A few matches later, the meet ended in a tie. I never forgot that match, for mine or at least one other teammate's victory would have made the difference between our team finishing alone in second place in the county instead of tied for second place. As I stood with my father afterward, Coach C. came up to us and slapped me on the back, repeating his view that I had indeed pinned my man.

The season ended and, finally, so did my senior year. I had managed to graduate second in my class, even placing first in mathematics. I had done well in several subjects, but there was something about math that fit my mind to a T. Although I'd find out in college that I wasn't as analytical as a top-notch mathematician needs to be, getting Bs in calculus and statistics, in high school, this weakness didn't manifest. Once I learned an algorithm, I could solve any problem given to me.

Salutatorian

"Did you really score 99 percent on your geometry Regents exam?" Mr. Nartowitz, the head of the math department, asked. I sat in his office, taking a twelfth-grade math exam.

"Yes," I answered, looking up to see him standing near me with a clipboard in his hand.

"And you scored a 96 in algebra, and I remember your 97 in trig." Mr. Nartowitz had been my teacher for both geometry and trigonometry.

I didn't know it at that time, but he and the faculty had just figured out that I would grab top math honors among the seniors that year. They may have been surprised for there were a few other students who were excellent mathematicians, including at least one girl (not unusual in 1971, but usually kept quiet or squelched because girls were still being discouraged from high achievement in math and science).

During my salutatory address at the graduation ceremony, I thanked the school for its support of a visually impaired student. I made a particular point of thanking my wrestling coaches who had supported a scholar-athlete with a disability.

This was not the speech I had planned to make. I thought that waxing philosophical about something (I hadn't gotten far enough in my thinking to figure out what) was more appropriate for the second smartest kid in the class. Instead, my father prodded me to use the speech as a vehicle to shine light on the needs and accomplishments of students with disabilities. I agreed to follow his suggestion because it seemed like the right thing to do, but not without some resentment.

At his urging, I'd already given up two scholarships. "The state is going to pay for your education, and you've already won a Regents Scholarship," he insisted. "Let someone else who needs it more have the money."

I was probably selfish in wanting to keep the money, but even more so, I wanted the glory. Perhaps I also wanted the pleasure of winning. It had been such a rare thing in my life, and here it was, my disability again, taking something away from me that I had accomplished despite that disability!

The salutatory speech forced me to face my disability in more than one way. There were the logistics of making my way to the podium. Then there was the fact I couldn't see what I'd written because the sun was in my eyes.

The ceremony was held on the football field. Students sat on bleachers facing west and into the late-afternoon sun. Family and friends sat on shaded bleachers facing east.

During rehearsal, I practiced walking from my seat to the podium until I'd memorized the number of steps. Had it not been for my father's foresight, I would not have known about the sun conditions until facing them in real time at the graduation ceremony. He took me to the site a few days prior to rehearsal to check things out and, even more insightful, at the same time of day the graduation would take place. Thus I was forced to memorize my speech.

Not since the blurring of my right eye in seventh grade had I felt so helpless because of poor eyesight.

Earlier that year, in fact before classes began, I had to do another thing I resented. I'd been admitted to an advanced placement English class. The class carried with it a large reading load. Despite my desire to sit and let come what may, my father galvanized me into action.

"Why haven't you contacted Recordings for the Blind (today, it is called Learning Ally) to get your books on tape?" he scolded. "What's the matter with you?"

"I don't want to go through the effort," I thought. My answer, "I don't know how," was also true.

"Call your teacher and get her to send you the list of books you will need. Then fill out this form (he handed me a piece of paper that had miraculously appeared) and send it in. Do it now, or you won't have your books on time."

I sprang into action.

This wasn't the first time my father had done his homework. Knowing my tendency to let things happen to me, he'd once again had to be the bad guy and kick me in the behind. In this case, he'd consulted with the itinerant teacher of visually impaired students, Mrs. Maglin, a woman who I'd spurned during ninth grade junior high school to avoid being even more mercilessly teased by the kids than I already was. Mrs. Maglin had worked predominantly with my younger brother Joseph, but was always at the ready to help me if needed. My father had simply followed her advice, "Contact Recordings for the Blind. They have college textbooks on tape."

Over the years, I've thought a great deal about my tendency to let things happen to me. Various people have offered different theories. My mother would say it is fatalism in concert with her belief that the world is an uncontrollable place and that what is meant to be is meant to be. For example, regarding death, she often intoned, "When your time is up, it's up." I've occasionally found comfort in this philosophy, for it removes from one's shoulders a portion of the burden of responsibility for his successes or failures. Sooner or later, however, the American ethos (rugged individualism) creeps in and with it guilt for not striving harder.

My father called me lazy. Deep inside though, I think he must have struggled with the paradox of seeing also how hard I played and how hard I worked. More likely, his use of that word covered up a deeper insight. His son was more than likely hyperanxious, occasionally paralyzed by it, or maybe even worse, depressed. I would someday understand the role of trauma in my emotional struggles, but for now, the struggles would continue.

Kelly Green and White

The following year, I commenced my higher education at Manhattan College in Riverdale, an upper-class neighborhood located in the northwest corner of the Bronx. It impressed me as a blend of city and country.

I learned about the school from Fred, a high school friend and elder brother of Tom, a classmate. Fred and Tom had roots in north Rockland County. Their family owned businesses and was involved in local politics. Fred and Tom helped me get my first two paying jobs, one, shoveling sludge along with them and the other, also with them, clearing trees to build a right-of-way road through property their family owned in Rockland County.

Fred and Tom's father was a doctor. Fred followed his father's footsteps, entering Manhattan College in 1970 as a premed student. Tom eventually became a lawyer, district attorney, and judge.

I conducted my search for an institution of higher learning in my senior year of high school. It centered on smaller colleges. They seemed more comfortable to the somewhat sheltered and shy seventeen-year-old thumbing through the college guide.

"Highly competitive," my father read. "You can handle that."

"Does the school have a dormitory?" I asked. I'd already decided that living away from home would be fun, having enjoyed my experience in Batavia three years earlier.

"Hamilton College appears to be a place where the students are serious," my father continued. "You should apply to that one."

"Where is it located?"

"Clinton. It's in upstate New York," he answered.

That seemed too far away, but I applied anyway, secretly hoping something else would come along.

Luckily, in early winter of 1970, Tom and I visited his brother Fred at Manhattan College. Manhattan offered tuition discounts to second children who attended, so Tom was pretty much set on going there. I was immediately impressed with two aspects of the campus. First, it seemed familiar, almost suburban, yet so close to the city that I knew there would be adventure. Second, there were hardly any women around. The school was technically an all-men's college at that point. Somehow, although I'd been around girls my entire education, their scarcity made me think there would be little distraction, just what I needed to get down to some serious studying. However, I wasn't disappointed when the school went coed the following year.

"We have a sister college," Fred informed. "The College of Mount Saint Vincent is about a mile up the road. It's a Catholic college, just like Manhattan. There are lots of priests and brothers here and lots of nuns up there. It makes it hard to get into their dorms," he chuckled.

I didn't care. The proximity to Yankee Stadium, which my family and I had driven past my entire life, and the smell of the Stella D'oro cookie factory wafting to my nose aided my comfort level. Besides, the school had a prelaw track, my goal as a high school senior, and a good liberal arts reputation. Also helpful was my experience in religious instruction and Sunday school classes in my youth, so the religious elements didn't frighten me. The fact that there were just as many Italian American boys at the school as Irish decreased any sense of cultural separation I might have imagined. My search was over.

With kelly green and white as its school colors and Jaspers as its nickname, Manhattan College is known for its great engineering, liberal arts, science, basketball, and track programs. In fact, many of the engineers who worked on the World Trade Center, both when it was originally built and in its unfortunate aftermath, were Manhattan graduates. Former Mayor Giuliani numbers among its alumni. I received a great liberal arts education there, deciding shortly after matriculation in September of 1971 to major in psychology.

Manhattan inaugurated a wrestling club during my sophomore year, but I didn't learn about it until the end of the season. Realizing how much I missed the sport and kicking myself for having remained idle for two seasons, I promised myself I would join the following fall.

In the meantime, I spent time with my dorm mates, some of whom ran track, lifting weights and running light workouts with them. With them, I learned to run five to six miles at full stride. Although I still retained sufficient vision to run without assistance, when unsure of my footing or on busy sidewalks, I rested my hand on the elbow of one of my running mates. By the time wrestling season started, I was well on my way to getting back into shape.

It was Joe, a dorm mate, who talked me into returning to wrestling. One evening in early spring of 1973, we wrestled in the hall of our dormitory. Despite the fact I hadn't done any serious wrestling in two years, I handled his moves quite well. Knowing that Joe had wrestled at only three-quarters' speed to preserve his strength for a tournament he'd be wrestling the following day didn't dampen my enthusiasm. Extrapolating to what would have happened had he been going full-tilt, my confidence was buoyed.

Dr. Bennet, the wrestling coach, taught physical education. His students called him Doc. In his day, he must have been a great wrestler. The first time I saw him demonstrate his skills in practice, it was against Tim, one of the best and quickest guys on our team. Doc gave him a run for his money.

Tim hailed from Olean, New York, a town not too far from Buffalo that suffered terrible floods in the early '70s. He and Joe were high school friends. Known affectionately as Mouse (probably because of the way his ears stood out), Tim was wiry and extremely fast. Over the next two years, he made it to the final round of most of the tournaments we entered.

In late October 1973, Doc called a meeting of prospective wrestling team candidates. After explaining that we would have "club" status on campus and would have to work out in a neighboring high school gym because the college did not have sufficient space, he further challenged our resolve by announcing in his best South Carolina accent, "I don't have time for this addition to my schedule." Gauging our reactions, he continued, "But if you are willing to work hard, so will I." This statement had the effect of instantly solidifying us into not only a team, but a band of brothers.

By now, my vision had begun to noticeably deteriorate. In class, I found myself struggling to see what was written on the chalkboard. I switched to felt-tipped pens for note-taking and used recorded books and volunteer readers for all but the most visually "mandatory" material (e.g., diagrams, pictures). Ancient and medieval art history classes, replete with slides of Greek and Egyptian statues, friezes, and Gothic cathedrals such as the Cathedral of Notre Dame eventually drove me to seek a waiver from such courses. However, for most of my undergraduate career, when I needed, I could still resort to a bright light and magnifying glass to look at a diagram or equation or, in the few science classes I took, laboratory instruments and specimens.

Getting around campus presented small but not insurmountable problems. I did not use a cane, having put away the one I was taught to use in Batavia a few years earlier. I had not needed it except for night travel, which I never did without being with someone. Besides, there was no way I was going to cause myself more taunting than I already absorbed from the kids in high school.

College life contained the task of walking quickly from building to building (some, such as the engineering building, were a few blocks away from main campus). Each trip had its mobility challenges for a visually impaired person. Some required trekking up and down irregularly spaced cement staircases. Other forays involved walking on paths and sidewalks dappled with bright sunlight and shadow. Many of the buildings were underlit, rendering me totally blind upon entering them from bright daylight. And then there was the city, which presented my archnemesis—the subway.

I managed to avoid the subway my freshman year. My high school friend Fred drove me home on weekends. Fred and I loved to heatedly debate topics ranging from birth control to the American presence in Vietnam. Unfortunately, a fight about money caused us to part company, and with the parting went my rides home on weekends. I scrounged rides from Fred's brother, Tom, and my father, but the handwriting was on the wall. I'd have to learn to get home on my own.

The final straw came in the form of an assignment from the medieval history professor to visit the Cloisters museum. I contacted my State counselor and requested mobility instruction. I was tired of being afraid of the subways, not to mention avoidance of night travel. With revamped cane skills, I hoped to have an easier time entering buildings from bright sunlight and be able to travel home on my own, not to mention the neighborhood bars!

Due to the slow progression of retinitis pigmentosa, one never knows how much eyesight has been lost until he tries something he hasn't done for a while. This time, returning to wrestling after a two-year layoff provided the needed information. I discovered that my vision had deteriorated to the point that I could no longer keep track of my opponent while we were in the neutral (standing) position. That may sound like a significant amount of eyesight to have lost in just two years and that I should have noticed it in other ways, but unless tested apples to apples and in action situations, one does not necessarily realize that it has occurred.

Fortunately, there is a rule that allows blind wrestlers to maintain fingertip contact with their opponents while they are on their feet. It is the responsibility of the referee to protect the blind grappler in case contact is broken. To the best of my knowledge, wrestling is the only mainstream competitive sport that contains standard rules for blind athletes.

Thus reluctantly and belatedly, I adopted the touch-start technique, although I never grew comfortable using it. Since the day I had taken my first opponent to the mat by circling and sizing him up, maintaining distance until the opportunity presented itself for a one- or two-step takedown lunge, the noncontact neutral position was in my blood. Thus the fingertip touch position left me feeling "handicapped." I assume my opponents felt the same, equally unaccustomed to the position, so that was some compensation.

In my first season on the Manhattan Wrestling Club, competition in certain weight classes was lighter than others, so it was not a surprise that I made the team. The club had not yet caught the attention of Manhattan College students, so some good wrestlers on campus had not come to the wrestle-offs (tryouts). However, we did have Augie, a wrestler in the lower weight classes who had placed second in the New York State high school championships, and Bob whose school had wrestled against mine in an annual winter holiday tournament and who was quite a good wrestler. Joe and Tim, also good grapplers, wrestled in the two weight classes just below mine.

Musings on Self-Image

Senior year brought with it my first encounter with the media, commencing the evolution of my attitude toward publicity. The *New York Times* approached me to do a story about a "special college wrestler." Perplexed that a prestigious paper like the *Times* would want to do an article about someone with only a .500 record, I refused the offer. A wrestler, I thought, even a blind one who didn't win more matches than he lost, was unworthy of special attention. Unwarranted publicity, especially if it exaggerated my accomplishments, would reinforce negative stereotypes and low expectations about blind people. ("Look how special he is.") I didn't want anyone to think that the only reason a moderately skilled wrestler had made the team was because he was blind. I had heard of a few blind wrestlers who competed in the mainstream and were true champions. They deserved the attention of a publication like the *New York Times*. I thought that allowing attention to me, an average wrestler, for the sake of a few minutes of fame would diminish their achievements.

Still, something nagged at me. Did I think so little of myself that I had devalued my own achievements? Was I not a blind wrestler competing against sighted guys on a mainstream team? Wasn't I the best that I could be?

My internal voice said no. I did in fact think I was underachieving. "Didn't you learn the truth about yourself at the Batavia program for the blind when the coach told you to get your act together, get into shape, and try harder?"

"But if true that I am an underachiever, couldn't at least some of it be attributed to my blindness? After all, everything I've done has been among totally sighted people, all the while trying to do so while under a handicap."

My internal debate hadn't sprung full-blown from my head. Even then, I was aware of the arguments among blindness educators about the best way to raise a visually impaired child. Some favored raising the child as I had been, in a totally mainstream environment. Others, the more old-fashioned, favored a segregated approach where the blind could live and grow among other blind people without "interference" from the sighted. Their belief was that imposing sighted norms on blind children impaired their overall development. Still, others favored a mixed approach where the child is raised in the mainstream, but special skills training and a healthy dose of interaction with blind peers is mixed in. This approach, it has been shown, provides ample opportunity for a blind child to learn about himself, the special skills he will need, and, very important, healthy social interaction. In this way, he can reach his highest potential.

Although I intuited all this at the time of the *New York Times* publicity offer, it would take years for me to fully understand these issues. In the meantime, with lots of ups and downs, I kept moving forward.

Glory Day

Over my entire career, my mother saw me wrestle only once. Luckily, I trounced my opponent. It was a match against Rockland Community College, not far from where I grew up. After the match, I strolled to where my family sat in the bleachers. My mother, clearly relieved, told me she'd held her breath until I lifted my opponent into the air and, under full control, place him on his back. Fortunately, my opponent was inexperienced, and I was able to dominate the entire match, never once causing her trepidation.

The only blemish to the victory was my failure to get a pin. This still intrigues me. I believe today, as I did when we grappled, that his shoulders were misshapen! It seemed that I had him in near-fall positions for most of the match. Once, after locking him up with a surefire pinning combination, the referee refused to call the fall. In exasperation, I simply got up and left him lying there. I strolled to the center of the mat, ceding him the "escape," and allowing him one of only a few points he'd earned that day. I don't think the rule-makers have ever considered requiring an anatomy check during the weigh-ins, but perhaps they should!

On that day, fortune was with me. I had come home and done well. Not only that, our team had won. Three other people who were important to me also watched that match. My father, who had seen me win and lose many a high school match, smiled as I approached to shake his hand. When my parents departed, a young lady I had been secretly dating (my parents didn't like her) sneaked up and gave me a big hug.

Finally, a former high school teammate, Jake, whose father, Mr. Daniels, had been our coach, slapped me on the back. "I thought that was you," I quipped. "No one has yelled at me like that since North Rockland."

"You weren't being tough enough on him," he retorted.

Jake had just completed a one-year stint at the US Military Academy at West Point. Always a great athlete, his toughness was fine-tuned there. On weekends, our friend Dennis and I drove his girlfriend, my cousin Angelyn, to visit him on the West Point campus. He would eventually marry her and go on to operate a successful carpet store and installation business in Rockland County. Their firstborn son graduated as a civil engineer from Manhattan College and their second son became a wrestling coach.

Years later, I would have another opportunity to come home and dazzle the hometown fans in an athletic competition. Fifteen years would have to pass and my second major athletic career ran most of its course before this glory day would come.

Head Case

"How did he do?" I heard the words but couldn't quite discern whence they came. It sounded like my dorm mate, Bill, hovering somewhere above me. "He did fine, but lost twice today. He's a lot better wrestler than that. I don't understand why he does so well in practice and doesn't win more matches." These words, spoken softly so I might not hear, sounded like those of Joe's, the teammate who, a year ago, had convinced me to sign up for wrestling. "I think he has problems with his head when it comes to competition."

Now I was sure I'd heard my friends. It was Saturday night in the winter of 1974, and I lay, facedown, on Joe's bed. I'd just returned from an hour-long stint in the bathroom where I'd discharged an evening's worth of beer. Unbeknownst to me, someone had spiked my final glass with vodka, a spirit my system hadn't been able to tolerate since I'd overindulged on screwdrivers two years earlier.

I had good reason for wanting to get drunk. Earlier that day, participating in a three-team multiple dual meet, I lost both my matches. In my first match, I ran up against a juggernaut. He shot in for a double-leg takedown and had me in his grasp before I could counter with a sprawl. (The sprawl involves pushing against the opponent's head and shoulders while shooting one's legs back and lowering one's hips.)

Lifting me into the air, the brute swiftly slammed me to the mat. The only reason he didn't put me down on my back and get a quick pin was because I had enough experience and presence of mind to torque my body. Thus instead of a quick finish, I landed prone, thus prolonging the torture. I had to keep on wrestling.

Struggling to my hands and knees, I felt myself enveloped by a wave of exhaustion. The match was only thirty seconds old. I thought, "How will I ever get through this? I don't want to be here." In effect, I'd already lost the match, having slid into "don't get pinned" mode.

At one point, Doc, tired of watching me merely "gutting" out the match, shouted, "Either stand up or sit out, but do something." I struggled off my belly, trying to fight back.

In the end, I avoided the pin but lost by a substantial margin. Returning to the bench, I noticed that only a few of my teammates came over to slap my back and comfort me. They tried to encourage me, saying, "You didn't let him pin you."

An hour later, in the final leg of the trifecta, I again found myself being trounced early in the match. Practically in tears, I angrily cursed myself for the feeling of hopelessness that had again swept over me.

Because I didn't want to hear my coach chastise me again, I tried hard to execute my favorite escapes. However, each time I stood up, my opponent threw me down; each time I sat out, he followed my hips and landed back on top of me. I didn't dare try a "switch," a reversal move, for fear of ending up on my back if improperly executed. I lost the match, but this time, when I returned to the bench, I was rip-roaring mad. Seeing this, my teammates kept their distance. Doc came up to me and said, "You fought hard, he just had you tied up from the beginning."

Later, reflecting on how I reacted to my coach's remonstration, I realized my father's harshness when growing frustrated with me as a boy might have been at play. Might his scolding have grown out of a realistic assessment that "tough love" would be an effective motivator? Doc seemed to have come to the same conclusion.

I first became aware of a tendency to "psych out," as we wrestlers called it, in the tenth grade. Wrestling is a grueling, full-body experience. It is easy to get tired and, given that your opponent is trying to bury your shoulder blades into the mat, hard to do anything but go full tilt full-time. As soon as the start whistle blows, you are on your toes, dancing, and shooting for a takedown. On the mats, your arms and legs power up to either maneuver or fend off your opponent. Your stomach, back, and neck muscles get strained in abnormal ways. Your mind expends energy to divert you from feeling pain from mat burns and muscle pulls you will become aware of only well after the match has ended.

My lifelong skirmish with occasional bouts of mental fatigue may have begun in infancy but was certainly exacerbated by an emotional trauma in tenth grade when my brother Lenny nearly died. It all began a few days before Christmas. Lenny and I as was our wont, spent a Sunday afternoon playing in the snow that blanketed our suburban neighborhood. We went sleigh-riding and engaged in snowball fights with our friends. I recall splattering a snowball on Lenny's chest, slinging it at him from close range. He may have swallowed a few morsels, but we were always breaking the rules and eating the snow, so I didn't think anything of it. Later that night, Lenny woke up with fever and all the signs of a bad cold. By midnight, his symptoms had worsened (throwing up, moaning, glassy-eyed, and pale-skinned) to the point that my father, with Lenny's consent, took him to the hospital.

The next morning, I went to school. We had a match against Washingtonville High School that afternoon, and I was wrestling on the junior varsity squad in the 138 pound slot. At a Christmas assembly that day, the entire student body sat in a darkened auditorium, listening to the chorus singing "Silver Bells." A tap on the shoulder and whispered words broke my reverie. "Anthony, please come to the principal's office now." Surprised, but not worried (I never broke school rules and didn't think I was in trouble), I followed the worker to the office. My aunt was there to take me home. Lenny had taken a turn for the worse. Somehow, he had contracted viral encephalitis. Because he had slipped into a coma, the doctors placed him on the critical list. They gave him three days to live.

We visited him at the hospital. He lay unclothed, his middle covered with sterile paper. Tubes emanated from his throat (tracheotomy) and arms. His eyes were open, fixed, and staring at the ceiling; the lights above dimmed. A respirator helped him to breathe.

When not at Lenny's bedside, we sat at home—my mother crying, my father angry, and my youngest brother Joseph seemingly too young to be aware of the gravity of the situation. I held on, saying to myself, "Don't get emotional until you have to. Save your strength." All the while, I wondered whether the snowball I had thrown at Lenny or some other snow he had ingested might have caused this catastrophe.

On Christmas Eve morning, we began taking down the decorated tree in our living room. Then the phone rang. My mother sobbed while my father answered it. "It's over," I said to myself, darkness descending over me.

In a moment, my father turned from the phone and announced, "He's awake, hungry, and asking for us!" As we clutched each other with tears gushing, I found myself believing once again in a God that, only a few days before, I had given up on for having forsaken my family.

Lenny did not emerge from his ordeal unscathed. The nasty virus left him with a temporary case of crossed eyes, a stomach ulcer from all the cortisone they gave him, and a noticeably shortened temper. He gained a lot of weight because of the bland diet they fed him afterward. All this, I feel, reduced his self-confidence. Today, he is a quiet and sometimes brooding bachelor who never left home. He lives with my mother, my father having passed away in 2008. If it weren't for his taking care of my parents, I would not have had the freedom to indulge my wander lust as much as I did. In his way, Lenny provided me with the foundation I needed to engage a higher-risk life path than I might otherwise have attempted.

As for me, it took twenty years, well after my wrestling career ended, to get over the trauma. For example, for two decades, I couldn't hear the song "Silver Bells" without crying. Moreover, I believe I absorbed the trauma by forming an association between it and anticipated athletic competition. Thus was created an avenue for anxiety to creep into my psyche every time a competitive match approached. This contributed to a tendency to grow prematurely fatigued.

For example, in eleventh grade, I competed in the mother of all junior varsity matches. The crowd had grown large in anticipation of the varsity meet that would follow when my match, well under way, caught their attention. A classic battle was taking place on the mats. Their eyes now focused, they commenced shouting my name.

My opponent and I sparred for the entire first period. Neither could take the other down. Both of us emerged huffing and puffing, arms and legs beginning to feel heavier. The score was 0–0. The crowd began to shout encouragement.

Because my opponent had won the coin toss, I was forced to assume the bottom position in the second period. The referee blew the whistle, and I stood up, broke my opponent's handhold, and spun around to face him, completing my escape. We spent the rest of the period dancing and lunging for a takedown. At the end of the period, both of us were growing quite fatigued. I led by a score of 1–0.

STAND UP OR SIT OUT

The opposing coach yelled, "He's all muscle (meaning no skill), you can beat this guy." I certainly didn't feel muscular at that moment, only increasingly exhausted.

Practically flopping into position atop my opponent to commence the third period and holding on to him with everything I had, I kept him down for nearly a minute before he slipped my grasp and escaped. The score was tied at one point apiece. The crowd noise (which I hadn't noticed to that point) grew deafening.

There we were: my two nemeses (fatigue and the opponent) and I, again face-to-face, standing, bending, dancing, and frothing at the mouth. We attacked each other repeatedly, trying to get the crucial takedown. My chest burned. My arms felt heavy as lead, and my legs felt like jelly.

When one passes the point of exhaustion, the world seems far away. The gymnasium, the crowd, Coach McGuire barking commands, my opponent, and indeed my body—all seemed surreal.

My opponent had a bit more energy than I, but he didn't know it. He smashed into me; I sat down on my rump and back-rolled out of bounds. The ref blew the whistle, and when I didn't pop right up, he walked over and dragged me back to the center of the mat. The hometown crowd screamed my name.

This time, my opponent, noticing my physical state, attacked more tactically. He hit me low on the legs, and I fell flat on my elbows and stomach. Even in semiconsciousness, a well-trained athlete knows how to fall. My opponent was awarded two points for a takedown.

The match was over. The score was 3–1. The buzzer sounded, and the crowd, appreciative of the enormity of the battle they had just witnessed, grew quiet. I crawled halfway to the bench. Again, the ref dragged me to the center of the mat for the final handshake and the raising of the winner's arm. We nodded at each other, both of us too tired to talk. The crowd, watching me barely able to walk back to my bench, broke into loud applause.

I walked slowly behind the bench to the warm-up mat and smelling salts I knew awaited me. I dropped onto my back. As I lay with my chest heaving, trying to catch my breath, my father's voice penetrated the buzz in my ears. "Pooped out again, didn't you?" His voice sounded both concerned and disappointed. But all I could hear was displeasure. There he was, even at this awful moment, scolding me again. My head involuntarily rolled back. Then snapping fully awake and forgetting my exhaustion, I stared straight at him and said nothing, thinking instead, "Someday, I'm going to kick your ass."

The coach came to my side. "Are you that out of shape?" In truth, I couldn't possibly have been "that out of shape." Or could I? For a moment I thought, "What would I have had to do to be that out of shape?" I'd practiced every day, lifted weights and ran during the off-season and played sandlot football and softball on weekends. Had I stopped putting out 100 percent during practices?

Shaking off the doubts, I centered my thinking on the severity of the ordeal I'd just been through. "These things happen," a teammate encouraged. "You did your best." Yet from that moment on, I wrestled every match, worried if I would get tired and lose. I know I was a good athlete, but from that point on, affairs of the head attenuated my output.

Speed

Watching Tim gave me the idea that I too could be fast. Speed derives from a concentrated burst of muscular output. For some, this comes naturally, and they can sustain rapid sequences of movement over long periods. For others (like myself), speediness can be trained.

"Just coil yourself and spring loose," Tim instructed at one of our college wrestling practices. "Have several moves in mind and practice going from one to the next without stopping. This will develop speed and stamina. Besides," he continued, "your first move might not work and unless you have another ready to try, you'll be tied up."

By my senior year in college, my stand-ups and sit-outs looked like blurs. However, I was inconsistent in employing them, so when I did, my teammates were happily surprised. I did eke out a few victories by using my speed and also managed to cause a friend to lose a match.

The scene was the warm-up mats at a community college tournament that our club was permitted to enter. The finals were often dominated by Suffolk CC which a number of New York State champions attended en route to four-year colleges. We had wrestled against Suffolk in a regular season match and lost almost all our matches. (As I recall, mine was one of the more respectable losses.)

As part of the warm-ups for the final, I assisted a fellow from Orange Community College in New Jersey. He had just beaten me in the previous round and, in a loose parallel to the Stockholm Syndrome, I had befriended him. During the warm-ups, I demonstrated my speedy sit-out, something I'd forgotten to do while wrestling against him. It worked beautifully.

"If you'd used that against me in our match," he scolded, "it would be me helping you warm up now."

Unfortunately, my friend's opponent was watching from the other side of the room. Sure enough, during their match, he used my moves to defeat the fellow from OCC. We never saw each other again.

Hanging 'Em Up

Graduation from college signaled my retirement from wrestling. This is the case for most collegiate wrestlers. There are few opportunities to continue in the sport after leaving the scholastic structure (unless of course you are a contender for the US national team or join one of a few amateur clubs begun by grappling die-hards who just can't give it up). Although in retrospect, I know it was time to end what had been a full career, begun in seventh grade, I would have liked to have won more matches. Nonetheless, I am content with what I had. There is little in life that compares to the fellowship of the team, the glory of the meet, the joy of contact, and the thrill of fast and powerful movement found in the sport of wrestling.

Interlude

I spent the years following my "retirement" from wrestling earning a master's degree, marrying Pat, dabbling in recreational sports, and much more. Pat was one of my readers in college and a woman who wouldn't give me the time of day romantically until well after we graduated. We began dating in 1975, and I convinced her to marry me in 1979. While we were married, I learned how to cross-country ski and, thanks to Pat, became a certified scuba diver.

With the exception of an advanced placement English course where I used tape-recorded books, I had never read printed material in any other way except visually. By the time I'd gotten to college, my vision had deteriorated a little, but more important, textbook-print size had decreased, and the volume of assigned reading seemed to have risen geometrically. Whereas in high school, I could get by reading my textbooks slowly and with a magnifying glass, in college, I was forced to figure out other ways to get my work done. Using human readers was one of those ways.

The state Commission for the Blind gave me a tape recorder. Recordings for the Blind (now Learning Ally), a great service, taped most of my textbooks so I could read them quickly and "eyes-free." Today, many blind students use optical character recognition (OCR) software to scan printed documents and read the documents on their PCs, which have been adapted with screen magnification or speech software. This technological combination is tantamount to having a reading machine. Today, many books are available in digital formats that can be downloaded and read on adapted computers, talking electronic notebooks, or smartphones.

However, in the 1970s, if, at the time I needed it, a book was still in the process of being recorded or if it was not slated for tap-ing at all, I recruited human readers. Money provided through the State Department of Education helped blind, and other "print-handicapped" students pay them.

Pat was an excellent and reliable reader. I met her in a class on, ironically, nonverbal communications, which was held at the College of Mount Saint Vincent, where she majored in biology. The Mount, as we affectionately called it, is a sister school to Manhattan College. When we met, Pat was a junior and a year ahead of me.

In addition to a few paperback books, the course required participants to engage in a yoga-like exercise class. One day, I must have appeared lost while exiting the gym. Noticing this, Pat pointed me to the exit and escorted me out of the building. As we walked to the bus stop for my return trip to Manhattan, joking and bantering, I knew immediately that I liked her.

I also thought she would make a great reader. However, when I asked her to record the books for our course, she balked. "You're kidding, right?" she answered. "No, I really have poor eyesight." I yammered. It took some convincing before she finally believed me. Years later, she told me, "I thought I was hearing just another line from a Jasper," the Manhattan College nickname.

Pat graduated and went on to the City University of New York to study for her PhD in biology. She was good enough to find a replacement reader, Greta, a fellow student at the Mount who I had the honor of taking to the Mount's senior prom.

In Pat's first year of graduate school (my senior year at Manhattan), we saw very little of each other. We spoke occasionally by telephone, catching each other up on our lives. She seemed happy. I didn't fully realize it, but I was lonely.

One Friday evening, late in spring, Pat called me from a phone booth a few blocks from campus. She asked if she could come up to the dorm for a visit. I was barely able to contain my excitement. Awaiting her arrival, I straightened my room and quickly spruced up. It was at that moment I finally admitted that I still harbored feelings for her.

When she arrived and stood in my open doorway, I couldn't believe my eyes. Pat had changed her hairstyle, and she looked prettier than I'd ever seen her. I'd always found her attractive, but now, nearly a year since I'd last laid eyes on her, I found her beautiful.

To my dismay, Pat didn't want to talk about us. Instead, she wanted to ask my advice. She told me about a love interest, asking me if she should or shouldn't pursue the relationship. I wanted to cry. Despite my disappointment, I gave her the most sincere and logical advice I could. I told her to forget him.

Despite the fact she left unhappy, I truly believe I gave her the proper advice. At some level, she knew it too; for despite her anguish, she eventually decided not to pursue the relationship. She also promised to keep in touch.

As soon as Pat walked out the door, I began pining for her, thinking of the long summer ahead and not knowing when or if I would hear from her. During those hot, lonely months, we corresponded by mail. I missed her even more. She visited friends in Virginia while I sat at home, doing little except waiting for graduate school acceptance and rejection letters.

A job I had held the past two summers had not come through again. I had worked as an assistant grounds keeper on the campus of a regional headquarters of the New York State Thruway Authority. In an act that might be considered employment discrimination today, the foreman, fearing I would get hurt crossing paths that occasionally included speeding cars from a squad of state troopers based there, openly refused to hire me back. The fact I had safely negotiated the campus, even agreeing to remain with my work partner at all times, and efficiently done the job the previous two summers did not impress him.

The day I received my letter of acceptance to Teachers College, Columbia University, was also the day a letter arrived from Pat, asking if we could see each other again. Spying the one from Teachers College and apparently ignoring the one from Pat, my dad walked into my bedroom where I sat reading a book and dropped two envelopes into my lap. Retrieving the one from Columbia University, he began to read, "It is our pleasure to inform you that you have been accepted to the master's degree program in rehabilitation counseling at Teachers College." Distracted by the unopened letter I held in my hand, I finally managed to comprehend what I had just heard. I whooped for joy. My first-choice school had come through.

My choice of programs and schools was a comfortable one. Because I'd met a few rehabilitation counselors, I had been influenced by their example. Also, my optometrist of many years, Dr. Paley, knew the director of the special education program at Teacher's College and had introduced us. We corresponded, and the director, perceiving my interests lay more in counseling than teaching, recommended me to the rehabilitation counseling program. The fact that attending a school located on the Upper West Side would keep me close to Pat also played a role in my decision.

Pat and I began dating that fall. It was 1975 and my first year of graduate school. Our sexy and intense romance kicked off with a camping trip at a State park in Putnam County, north of New York City. She taught me about feminism. She told me that there was no way she would ever take the name of a man if she were to get married. She also taught me how to be adventurous. Several months later, for example, she and another couple "kidnapped" me on Valentine's Day for a romantic stay in an upstate hotel. We fell in love.

During the summer of 1976, our nation's bicentennial and between my first and second years of graduate school, Pat and I suffered three months' separation. While she took a field course at the University of Michigan's Upper Peninsula, I took a summer job at Camp Jawanio, a program for severely physically disabled children and adults in New City, about thirty miles northwest of New York City and about ten miles south of West Haverstraw.

The separation was painful. We worked so hard (about twelve hours per day) we barely had strength to write. While I pushed boys and men in wheelchairs, lifting, dressing, bathrooming, doing physical therapy, counseling, and spending an enjoyable time with them, Pat learned how to identify and skillfully observe animals in the wild. Once a week, I bullied my way to one of only two pay telephones available to us counselors. Pat had a similar task. My aunt, who worked for the telephone company, connected us for our all-too-brief conversations. When we reunited, we celebrated the bicentennial with plenty of fireworks.

The experiences we had were well worth the separation. I made strides toward becoming a better rehabilitation counselor, and she a skilled field biologist.

Graduating in 1977, it took me six of the most painful months of my life to secure my first job offer. I enlisted the assistance of a placement specialist, my friends and family, and all the business contacts I had made while a graduate student. Most of the rejections seemed genuine. "We really need someone with more experience," several interviewers told me.

A few appeared to reject me as soon as they saw my cane. "Here, look at this medical report," an interviewer challenged. "How will you read this?"

"I'll use a magnifying device," I answered. "If that doesn't work, I'll use a reader."

"We can't provide you with a reader," she persisted.

"Then I'll get my own."

In 1977, Section 504, the antidiscrimination portion of the Rehabilitation Act of 1973 was known to mainstream employers who did business with the federal government and should have been known to anyone in the rehabilitation field, the sphere in which I was seeking employment. The Americans with Disabilities Act (ADA) was still thirteen years away. In those days, I found more overt discrimination in my own field than anywhere. Perhaps people in the business suffered from a form of "compassion fatigue," I thought. Although job discrimination against people with disabilities still exists in all occupational realms, it is less tolerated today than in those days.

Things got so bad my father, in an effort to maintain my morale, proposed a situation for me as a hot dog stand operator in West Haverstraw. I politely declined. A few weeks later, I received an offer.

Actually, I received two offers, one right after the other. The first came from the State University of New York at Farmingdale. I went so far as to put a deposit down on an apartment in Nassau County, on Long Island, fully expecting to go to work as a job placement specialist for college students with disabilities. I accepted the position because to my shock, in the six months since beginning an intense job search, this was my first bona fide offer.

There were downsides. The position was funded by a three-year federal grant with only a promise that the college would try to pick up the salary after it expired. The fieldwork portion of the job would be difficult because I didn't drive. At that time, public transportation was sparse in central Long Island. Even worse, I dreaded the thought of being so far from Pat.

While waiting for Farmingdale to give me a contract, I received an offer from the New York State Commission for the Blind and Visually Handicapped, now called Commission for the Blind. The position, vocational rehabilitation counselor trainee, brought with it three things. First was the power and, by default, the prestige that comes with being able to wield the state purse strings to purchase services for my clients. Second was the fact I would report to work in the Harlem State Office Building. This meant I would be in familiar territory. Only a fifteen-minute walk from Teachers College, its location in Manhattan meant I could live part-time with my parents and part-time with Pat until I got settled. Third, although the starting salary was about 10 percent less per year than Farmingdale's, I knew the position had stability and that my salary would steadily rise over the years.

I dumped Farmingdale in an admittedly clumsy manner. Competition for the position had begun with three hundred applicants. After two rounds of interviews, my prospective supervisor later confided I had impressed a lot of people. When, just as the school was about to mail me a contract, I told him I wouldn't be accepting the offer after all, he was quite upset. Years later, I learned that I had made the right move. The position was abolished after the three-year grant expired. Thankfully, since reporting for work with the commission in late December 1977, I was not unemployed for more than a few months in between jobs until retirement.

Now began the job of learning my job. The commission provided me a closed circuit television (CCTV) magnification device, and my supervisor, an experienced and clinically astute former counselor herself, trained me in the intricacies of the state bureaucracy.

She taught me how to quickly size up clients, verify my hypotheses by truly getting to know them, and how to set up and monitor services they would need to become "rehabilitated." Rehabilitation, she told me, meant helping our clients develop a sense of well-being as much as it did developing compensatory skills, with employment the ultimate outcome.

Although the CCTV helped, I needed human readers to do most of my voluminous paperwork. While as a college student, the state had paid for my readers, in 1977, it did not yet fund readers for its employees.

I called upon a blind colleague who had lots of connections in the community and solicited his help to find volunteer readers. He gave me Bob.

Bob was a retired businessman and dirty limerick-spouting raconteur ("There once was a woman from Regina...") who lived in upper Manhattan. We worked together for fifteen years, becoming close friends. He had a fascinating story. Born in 1915, he grew up in Lincoln, Nebraska, obtained a law degree, and, in 1940, the winds of war whistling loudly, enlisted in the Army. He was a fully aware, but closeted homosexual.

On December 7, 1941, Bob went into town and sat in a movie theater with fellow enlistees, enjoying newsreels and entertaining films. Suddenly, the screen went dark, the lights came up, and an officer ordered all soldiers back to base. A squad of military police lined up at the back of the theater to enforce the order. The officer told everyone in the theater that the Navy base at Pearl Harbor, Hawaii, had just been bombed by the Japanese. Sensing he would be in the Army for a long time and already well-educated, Bob signed up for Officer Candidate School. He eventually became a captain, serving in the Quartermaster Corps in the European theater. His standing joke was that he started in one theater and ended up in another!

When the war ended, Bob left the Army and joined the State Department. He served as liaison between the American and British sectors of the then-partitioned Germany. He loved this work and did it well until someone in officialdom learned of his homosexuality. As was the custom in those days, Bob was asked to resign his position with the State Department for fear that he might be vulnerable to blackmail by the "enemy"—in this case, the Communists. He reluctantly did so, joining the Better Business Bureau in New York City where he enjoyed a successful thirty-year career, retiring in 1977 at age sixty-two. In the meantime, because of the kind of man he was and because it was necessary, Bob took responsibility for raising his nephew, sending him to a quality preparatory school in New York, seeing him through graduate school and on to a fine career as a scientist.

Bob assisted me with job-related paperwork all the way to 1992, when his health began to deteriorate.

In 1979, after a year's delay while we watched the painful process that ended with Pat's father dying of lung cancer, Pat and I married. We had wanted to tie the knot several months earlier, but her parents, reluctant to put her father through the ordeal, asked us to wait. We argued that it would be nice for her father to see his daughter get married, but by then, he was no longer able to walk. The dream of escorting her down the aisle had dissolved. The lung cancer had metastasized to his brain, disabling some of his motor centers, and despite our enlightened argument that there would be no embarrassment if he used a wheelchair, they demurred. At our wedding, Pat's paternal uncle saw to it that she made it to the altar.

We honeymooned in St. Thomas and Puerto Rico. When we returned, we wasted no time in learning how to play with our newest toy, a canoe given to us by my brothers as a wedding present. A sleek fiberglass craft, sixteen feet in length, the bright-red canoe was ideal for paddling on lakes in the Adirondacks and even on the Hudson River. No one taught us how to handle the craft. We jumped in and just began stroking. Later, we took a few lessons, and I learned how to J-stroke and that paddling too vigorously was counterproductive. The harder I pumped, I learned, the more the bow seemed to sway from left to right and then back the other way as I tried to undo the damage! Pat would call back from her perch in the bow, "Take it easy, muscleman. You're doing a whole lot of nothing back there."

The most valuable lesson we learned was to routinely look up at the sky to check the weather. It was especially important to look over our shoulders. Once, while on the Hudson, a squall came up on us from behind so quickly we found ourselves enveloped in high wind and heavy spray before we could paddle away from the middle of the river. We were hit broadside with waves to the point where we thought we would surely capsize. Our solution: turn our backs to the wind and paddle at an oblique angle with all we had toward shore. In this way, the wind pushed us in the direction we needed to go, and the spray was out of our faces. The other lesson we learned was to make sure no large ships or barges headed in our direction got too close!

Pat and I lived in a small one-bedroom apartment on the first floor of a house in north Yonkers. The upper floor was occupied by our landlords, a Chinese couple with two college-aged sons. For some reason, their names, at least in English, were the same. I don't know why, but judging from the gaudy red wallpaper in our kitchen, I doubt if our landlords were sufficiently Americanized to be imitating George Foreman! Perhaps the boys had different names in Chinese. If so, we never found out.

The house was located on Pine Street. We lived there for two years before learning that just before we moved in, David Berkowitz, the serial killer who had terrorized the New York-Metropolitan area for several months, had been captured only a few feet from our driveway. Better known as Son of Sam, or the .44 Caliber Killer, Mr. Berkowitz had lived in an apartment building just down the block. The building was positioned uphill from the home of Sam Carr, owner of the dog that supposedly gave Berkowitz his hallucinogenic orders. The former postal worker would often look down at the dog playing in Sam Carr's backyard and, apparently, imagining that the dog had instructed him, would head out to kill people. No wonder our rent was so low! Eventually, we moved into a large two-bedroom apartment in a nice building a few blocks away.

In 1980, I gave in to the lure of academia. Pat had earned her PhD in biology and secured a teaching position. Watching her prepare lectures, occasionally lending her a hand with laboratory and field research, and interacting with her doctoral-level colleagues made me long to crack the books again. I believed that with Pat's experience and support, I could earn the coveted sheepskin. I audited a course at Teachers College in the spring of 1981 and found the mix of school and work palatable. I applied to doctoral programs in counseling psychology. In May, three and a half years after I launched my career as a rehabilitation counselor, I called my dad to tell him I'd been accepted into two programs and had chosen the PhD program at NYU.

Becoming "Doctor Candela" was a dream my father had for me since I was a precocious first grader showing early academic promise. Despite poor eyesight, I'd won reading awards and generally did well in school. By the time I was a sixth grader, my father prophesied that I would become a lawyer. By mid–high school, he had broadened his prediction to include any doctoral-level degree; he didn't care which. He, more than anyone else, was the driving force behind my early academic success, encouraging me not to feel sorry for myself because I was visually impaired.

On the phone, we shed tears of joy, convinced we would ultimately get our wish that I earn a PhD. I embarked on what turned out to be an eleven-year venture, thoroughly enjoying the experience of learning a subject in depth and developing the type of discipline that renders people worthy of calling themselves "doctor."

Into the Deep

> Sank through easeful
> azure. Flower
> creatures flashed and
> Shimmered there lost
> images
> fadingly remembered.
> Swiftly descended
> into canyon of cold
> nightgreen emptiness.
> Freefalling, weightless
> as in dreams of
> wingless flight…
>
> —"The Diver" by Robert Hayden

In 1981, Pat signed up for a marine biology expedition and needed to learn to scuba dive. She asked me to take the class with her. Despite my love for the water (I'd learned to swim before I was ten years old), I had my doubts. "I'm afraid they won't want a visually impaired person in their class," I complained.

When I was a child in day camp swim class, I had sufficient eyesight to see the coach demonstrate how to flutter kick and the proper way to execute a crawl stroke. I was fairly certain I could no longer learn that way.

"We'll do it together," Pat encouraged. "We've figured out how to do other things," she added. "Besides, you are a good swimmer and a natural under water."

I explained my situation to the diving instructor. I proposed we would develop special techniques as we went along. To my surprise, he gave us the "thumbs-up." All he had to say was, "That will be very fine," and we knew things were going to be all right. We learned to dive.

The instructors got into it too. They were fascinated by the hand-over-hand instruction they watched Pat providing me. Under their careful eye, I learned how to don and handle a wet suit, air tank, regulator, fins, mask, snorkel, gauges, buoyancy control vest, and sundry items including the lanyard that exploded a gas canister into your vest for emergency ascents.

With several hours of classroom instruction and a textbook (Pat was my reader again), we learned how to calculate how deep it was safe to go and how long we could stay down there before either running out of air or risking the bends. (Today, divers have underwater computers to help them do what we had to do using charts, pencil, and paper.) Lessons about the physiology of humans under multi-atmospheric pressures, techniques of controlled ascent, the diving industry, and more rounded out our training.

We undertook our open-water certification dive in a flooded rock quarry in northern New Jersey. The twenty-five-foot deep water-filled quarry contained a sunken boat and Volkswagen "bug" for divers to play with. In those days, I still had enough vision left to see the car and boat through the clear fresh water while floating on the surface, mask facing down and snorkel pointing up.

With regulator in mouth, I pressed a button on my buoyancy control vest (BCV), releasing most of the air that partially filled it. Pat tugged on my arm and, as rehearsed in the training pool, we gave each other the "descend" signal (thumbs-down). Pointing our torsos downward, legs together and knees bent, we performed synchronized dolphin kicks that thrust us down into the depths. Scissor-kicking and releasing air from the BCVs, our fifteen-pound lead weight belts overcame the remaining buoyancy caused by our bodies, tanks, and wet suits. We swam toward the boat, touching down on its bow.

Crawling to the cabin and making sure Pat knew what I was about to do by showing her my hand in the "okay" position, I stuck my head inside. Suddenly, I felt a tug on my leg and heard Pat's voice clearly shout, "No!" The diving instructors taught us that water is a great conductor of sound. If you take a deep breath and spit out your regulator, you can actually shout a word or two and still keep enough air in your chest to clear your regulator when placing it back in your mouth.

Pushing back, I emerged from the hole. Grabbing my hand, Pat signaled me to surface with an upward thrust of her thumb.

Swimming to the surface, filling our BCVs directly from our tanks as we rose, we popped through the surface and spit out our regulators. "What's the matter?" I asked somewhat indignantly. "You were about to get stuck in that hole," Pat retorted. "Don't you know your tanks are a lot thicker than you are?" This gave me sufficient pause to never try underwater spelunking again.

Our saltwater certification exam took place in early May in the Long Island Sound. The water at that time of year supports temperatures of only about fifty-five degrees. We entered the briny deep dressed in full wet suits including gloves and hoods.

Diving from a boat, which we boarded on City Island, just east of the Bronx, the Sound greeted us with murky water and a muddy bottom. Visibility was only the length of an arm. Crawling in the mire, all the while making sure I kept Pat close to my left side, I managed to find buried treasure. The treasure came in the form of a very old Budweiser bottle. I didn't learn about the antiquity of the bottle until we surfaced, but while we crawled in the ooze, Pat did manage to finger-spell the letters, B-U-D into my gloved hand. When foolishly I began to laugh, I nearly choked to death. The instructors hadn't taught us how to continue to breathe through a regulator while engaged in comic relief.

I contemplated removing the bottle to the surface, a souvenir of our adventure, but Pat convinced me otherwise. Ever the biologist and not wishing to disturb the delicate ecology of the Sound, she "persuaded" me to let the Budweiser bottle remain within its mucky sepulcher. A sharp slap on my wrist ensured that the vessel would remain mired in the mire in perpetuity.

In 1982, I published an article in the prestigious *Journal of Visual Impairment and Blindness*, the recording arm of the American Foundation for the Blind, on how blind people dive with scuba (self-contained underwater breathing apparatus). I described the system of tactual hand signals that Pat and I invented to notify me of the air pressure remaining in my tank. For example, Pat read the gauge during a routine check. Then she pounded her (usually gloved) fist into my palm, once for each one hundred pounds of available air. Likewise, each thrust of fingers, held straight and firm, represented ten pounds of air. Other signals, such as the "okay" (thumb and forefinger formed into a circle), the "ascend" (thumb up) and "descend" (thumb down) are the same used by all divers. I just needed to touch the hand that made them.

Once we dived in the Caribbean. Taking a chartered boat to about ten miles off the Puerto Rican shore, we and a group of tourists descended to a wrecked Spanish galleon. The boat had sunk about seventy-five feet to the bottom nearly one hundred years before. Because the ship was almost completely encrusted in coral, only its vague boatlike shape and an exposed stern and anchor assured us a ship really lay under all that coral.

Years later, I dived with the Moray Wheels, a club dedicated to divers with disabilities and based in Boston. It was with "the Wheels" that I took my deepest dive (ninety feet into a canyon in the Atlantic off the Massachusetts coastline). The water was very cold, and I recall seeing nothing at all on that dive. In fact, while trying to descend, I temporarily lost touch with my diving buddy, a fellow whom I had met only an hour earlier. Instructed to float feet down just under the waves, we released just enough air from our BCVs to remain buoyant at five feet beneath the surface. I couldn't see that I had sunk below everyone else. Afraid to descend alone, I hung there, probably only ten feet lower than the rest of the group, and waited. My buddy, unable to find me and growing impatient, broke a cardinal rule. He descended without me. Quickly realizing his error, he retreated and located me. Signaling each other to descend, we flipped over and vigorously swam straight down.

We touched down on a ledge at ninety feet. My partner placed my hands on shells and strangely shaped rocks. I marveled at how far down we sat. I had no sense of the boat or sky above me; I could make out only uniform blur. More experienced divers descended off the ledge into murky darkness and down to 150 feet. One of the nondisabled divers in our group returned to the ship so giddy, we feared he'd come down with a case of "raptures of the deep" (nitrogen narcosis). He was merely elated.

My most interesting dive, admittedly tame by diving standards, was into the great tank at the Boston Aquarium. Arranged by the Moray Wheels, the controlled circumstances of this dive enabled our small group to play with a manta, touch sand sharks, and ride the back of a mama sea turtle. If not for the physical and hand-over-hand assistance of the aquarium divers who accompanied us into the twenty-five-foot tank, most of us would never have gotten so close to these marine animals. Well fed and approachable if done carefully, these aquatic beings would have forever remained invisible to me if not for the Moray Wheels.

In 1986, I was invited to speak in Miami at a conference on scuba diving for people with disabilities. This was my inauguration into just what writing an article could do for you. Publicity from my scuba piece in the *Journal of Visual Impairment and Blindness* landed me an all-expense-paid trip to speak on a panel with two other blind divers. Steeped in my doctoral studies in psychology, my topic focused on the role of anxiety in diving for blind persons. I spoke about some of the stress I felt being unable to see my bubbles (the preferred method for knowing which direction is up and which is down during periods of disorientation at depth), worry about the skill of new diving buddies, and primeval fears conjured by descending into virtual nothingness. The latter topic seemed to draw murmurs, as if I had breached a taboo. Either my perspective was piercingly insightful, I thought, or I had bared my soul a bit too much.

My talk contained lighter elements. The audience seemed to resonate to my description of the thrill of swimming in all three dimensions and enjoying the kinesthetic sensations. They were particularly tickled when I likened the experience to that of an astronaut in outer space (a fantasy I have harbored since a little boy).

My copanelists talked about the mechanics of diving without sight and their favorite diving experiences. The deaf divers, normally sighted and skilled in sign language, complained about difficulties in passing the written certification exam. Divers with physical impairments spoke about and demonstrated alternative propulsion, buoyancy, and weighting apparatus. Alternative methods of propulsion included water wings for those who used arm power instead of their legs and underwater scooters for the quadriplegics who strapped themselves to machines that they maneuvered using head controls. Needing little provocation to race, they could gleefully outrun us so-called able-bodied divers. Laden with flippers on our feet and gluteus maximus muscles that got most of their exercise in deck chairs, we who were gifted with leg power marveled at the speed, agility, and freedom the scooters provided their users. Amazingly, people with asthma and other lung conditions spoke of the freedom they felt under near-weightless conditions and breathing the extremely clean air pressure-pumped into SCUBA tanks.

Moving On

Just when you think your life's path has finally been set and your carefully laid plans have begun to bear fruit, things change. Even in hindsight, one can never know for sure which path would have been the best one; each has its own benefits and downsides. A timely step in a place one might never have trodden might be worth more than a large step in a familiar locale. We can do know more than to take what life gives us and to move on.

Because the counseling psychology program at NYU catered to employed students, I was able to take late-afternoon and evening classes there while continuing to work full-time. The program's philosophy melded nicely with my own. It emphasized the psychology of the "normal" person, focusing on developmental life stages and acknowledging "differentness" as part of normalcy. This, in a nutshell, has been my life's quest.

As a professional dedicated to working with people with disabilities, I believed I needed to understand how differentness and "normalcy" could be melded together. I yearned to extend the metaphor of the "melting pot," imperfect and potentially alienating as it might be, down to the psychological level. Today, I subscribe to more of a "beef stew" or "salad" philosophy, one that allows people with differences to coexist in such a way that they can come together in society and yet retain their uniqueness.

Unfortunately for my studies, not to mention life in general, in 1983 things between Pat and me began to deteriorate. This was quite a blow, for I truly thought she and I would be together forever. Not only that, I had counted on her long-term support to help me get through a decade of full-time employment and part-time study ahead of me. Moreover, I had mixed feelings about the prospect of being single again. Yes, I would have my own space, and "singlehood" would allow me to get into the "hunt" for beautiful women again, but performing the chores of everyday living without Pat's help would take more time from my day and leave me less time for study. Nonetheless, despite the fact we had waited until our late twenties to marry (a mature time by most estimates back then), Pat and I had slowly come to realize that we needed more than our married life provided. Perhaps we were not as mature as we thought.

In April 1983, Pat left me alone for a week with the cat while she attended a biology conference. As it turned out, we both did a lot of thinking. Realizing that we had enjoyed our time apart, pretending, at least in our minds, to be single again, by the time she got home, we had tacitly accepted the fact that we were on the road to separation.

We had little time to process the daunting revelation. A day after Pat's return, a fire devastated half our Yonkers apartment building. This proved to be the final straw; our marriage was collapsing, and life's exigencies were conspiring to put an end to it.

Fortunately, in terms of our safety, we had just been through a fire scare a month earlier and were ready to act when we heard cries from the hall for people to evacuate. Grabbing the cat, our coats, and wallets, we quickly made sure the lights, computer, TV, and stove were turned off and ran to the parking lot to retrieve the car. It was a good thing we did, for when it was over, our parking space lay under a pile of rubble.

The fire had started, we later learned, in an apartment with a short-circuiting electrical wire. The tenants tried in vain to snuff the fire with a mattress, which then also combusted and spread flames throughout their apartment. Unbeknownst to everyone until days later, another electrical fire had also started inside the wall. The combined effect of the two fires caused the rapid demise of a large chunk of the building. Luckily, the portion of the building where our apartment stood escaped all but a little smoke damage.

The trauma of standing in front of our building watching flames slowly engulf it proved quite life-changing. Although the trucks arrived quickly, it took an inordinate length of time for the water pressure to build up enough for firefighters to begin to dowse them. While we waited, the flames moved up and down the building and from front to back. Pat and I ran to the rear to help neighbors climb down the fire escapes. One of our friends, after making her way to the ground, bemoaned the fact she had left her oven on. We told her not to worry. "The fire will be out in a few minutes, and you'll be back in your apartment," I reassured. I was terribly wrong. By the time we were ordered out front again, the building was in the hands of a power far beyond us.

Pat and I got into our car and drove north to my parents' home. While she cried and my mother comforted her, I reported to my father that I thought our apartment had the best chance of any to survive.

The next day, we returned to find that our apartment was unscathed. While one side of the building had disintegrated, the other side remained completely intact. Fire officials allowed us to enter under escort. We noted the surprising lack of damage, collected our Apple II Plus computer and parakeets, packed a suitcase with clothing and work materials, and returned to my parents' house in West Haverstraw and my old room. The three-week evacuation placed enough stress on our already-unraveling marriage to cause us to do some serious soul-searching. By the time we reentered our home, we had agreed to go our separate ways.

In early 1984, I was on my own for the first time. Over the previous year, I had fantasized about having my own apartment. Except for dormitory living, I had never lived alone. The bachelor life had a certain allure, but so long as I was safely married, I could easily suppress thoughts about the downsides. Now, having gotten what I wanted, I was lonely and depressed. Casting about, I did the thing I do best: put one foot in front of the other, hung in there, and waited for things to get better.

The pain of separation from Pat was surprisingly excruciating. I missed her presence. She had so thoroughly entwined herself in my being that I could not imagine living without her. She was inside me in ways I had not thought about since we began dating eight years earlier.

In the first few months of our separation, while we decided whether to divorce or not, Pat missed me as much as I missed her. Fearful to venture out too quickly, she occasionally dropped by my apartment or I visited hers for dinner and an evening of pseudo romance. These liaisons lasted nearly six months. The inevitable finally happened. When she called to tell me it was truly over, that she had found someone new, and that she wanted a divorce, it felt as if I had been shot.

I was mired in the mourning process for nearly two years. Catching me unawares, people noticed my head drooping in sad reverie. I dreaded the weekends, knowing I would be alone with only my thoughts and feelings. Compulsively, I sought the company of women. It didn't take long to decide that I also needed the help of a therapist.

Seeking out a psychologist colleague, I confided, "I can't go on like this. The pain is just too much." He gave me a referral to an Upper West Side therapist. "You are in a lot of pain," he empathized. As we shook hands and I prepared to leave his office, he concluded our session by saying, "Try to remember, this too shall pass."

He was right. After a while, the pain began to subside, and I didn't feel the same level of desperation. Bachelor life assumed a calmer, more normal rhythm. Time and therapy helped. My first task was to stop feeling guilty for the dissolution of my marriage. Taking stock of the things about myself that contributed to my breakup with Pat, I reluctantly admitted that my bête noire was anger. I fell back into the depths of despair. How could I rise above something that was so deep-seated that it sprung upon me when I least expected it? How could I avoid the tantrums and fights that had eroded my marriage? Vowing that if I ever got into a long-term relationship again, I wouldn't make the same mistakes, I put my faith in time and therapy and moved on.

Things changed. My head no longer drooped. Close friends pointed out that I had even stopped compulsively seeking the company of women. Indeed, there were weekends when I had gone out on as many as three dates. This was a timely decision as the AIDS epidemic had already begun its rampage. Regaining the ability to be alone with my thoughts and feelings could not have come at a better time.

End of the War

Since the day I learned that I would have to wear eyeglasses "forever," the thought conjured profound ambivalence. I hated them, wanted to lose them, tried to break them, and yet without them, I couldn't see well enough to walk safely, read, catch a ball, or even keep my eyes open for long periods. I must have repressed the anger I felt toward them for, although I never lost the yearning to be rid of them, eyeglasses had become an inescapable part of me.

In my early thirties, optical aids (eyeglasses, magnifying glasses, binoculars, telescopes) had begun to lose their effectiveness for me. It was clear that my eyesight was deteriorating. In response, at age thirty-two, in one of the most proactive moves I've ever made, I learned to read braille. I later joked that I saw the handwriting on the wall, and realizing I really could not see the handwriting on a wall or anyplace else, I'd better learn a new way to read.

Once a week, I met with a skilled braille instructor. At first, the process of learning to read and write was difficult. Tactually discerning the individual braille dots was nearly impossible. Memorizing the various configurations of the six dots comprising the braille cell was not hard; recognizing the tactile symbols turned out to be the difficult part. To this day, I am a slow reader of braille. Mine is a typical case. Although I am much faster today, I've never gotten as fast at reading and writing braille as people like my brother Joe who learned it at a younger age.

After three months, having memorized the code, I could read slowly and write with a mechanical braille "typewriter." A handheld metal slate and stylus provided another, albeit tedious, way to write. Today, most of us use electronic "refreshable braille devices that store large amounts of information, are lightweight, and often come coupled with synthetic speech.

When, as a young adult, the notion that I would someday be blind fully coalesced in my mind, it occurred to me that there just might be a point along the way where eyeglasses would no longer be helpful. In my imagination, I would awake one day to an epiphany: The day had finally come; my eyeglasses were no longer needed. I would engage in a ceremonial ablution, a cleansing of the noxious humor that had permeated my psyche since I was a toddler.

My imaginary plan called for taking my spectacles to a brick wall and, standing a few feet from the rock-hard surface, slamming them into it with all my might. I then imagined myself engulfed in a warm feeling of liberation. Free at last, I take my cane in hand, pat its handle much as cowboys pat their horses in old Western movies, and stride triumphant into the sunset.

Arriving home, I look into a mirror and see not my present face, but my face as it appeared in the photo taken when I was two and a half years old and before I started wearing glasses. This was the photo that upset me so much when I first saw it, perhaps a year after it was taken. At that tender age, I knew my life would never be the same again. In my fantasy, seeing my old face in the mirror fills me with the feeling that I have found myself.

The day of reckoning finally did arrive. Only there was no epiphany. Over the past few years, my acuity had become so poor that I was unable to read books, my notes, or even my wristwatch without a struggle. I had begun to see after images and thought the lenses might be the cause.

One morning, I put on my glasses; and noticing the effect of the after-images more vividly than ever, I closed my eyes and removed the glasses. Holding my breath, I opened my eyes, and the afterimages were no longer there. My vision was clearer; the acuity was terrible, but not much worse than when wearing the glasses.

Convinced spectacles were no longer the answer, I resolved to do without them. Now, for sure, I would need to dive into braille and find other ways to read and write.

Yielding up one's crutches, no matter how poor their service has been lately, does not come without some doubting and discomfort. Was I making a mistake? Should I go one more time to a low-vision optometrist to obtain a new prescription? Was my desire to rid myself of the nemesis clouding my judgment? "If I fight the good fight just one more time," I mused, "I won't feel as though I've given up too soon."

Shaking myself free of the vicious circle I was slipping into, I resolved, "It's time to go cold turkey." I took a deep breath, holding my glasses in my fist. The image of obliterating them loomed clear. I felt their texture and began to squeeze. I faltered. Much as a child unable to hurt a kitten upon a dare, the thought of hurting the object in my hand suddenly filled me with shame. What had my glasses done all these years except try to help me? Was it their fault they couldn't give me something I didn't possess naturally?

"No," I said aloud. "Enough is enough." The fragile orthotics, appendages to my eyes and occasionally, a burden to my nose, didn't deserve the violent end I had planned for them any more than I deserved not to see well. The thirty-plus years' war was over. Images of their destruction dissolved into tears. Bidding them farewell, I gently placed the glasses into a case and, shutting the night table drawer, closed a chapter in my life.

"Most people don't have a chance like this," I told my therapist. She had just heard the saga of the eyeglasses and wanted me to think of something positive I could take with me into the next phase of my life.

"I imagine most people experience the end of something as long-standing as my relationship with eyeglasses as a true finish. They probably imagine themselves blind and hopelessly at sea. What good would it do to ferret among the ashes? There's no material there with which to rebuild."

"Do you really feel that way?" she asked.

"No," I answered. "I guess I've got a lot to carry forward, don't I?"

"What will you carry forward?"

"That's easy," I said. "I'll carry all the experience and memory of vision. I also have a great deal of experience compensating for lack of vision."

"Actually," I thought, growing expansive, "I'm well-equipped because I've been preparing for blindness all my life. It is by no means as scary or devastating as I thought it would be."

"Do you remember how you felt when you first broke up with Pat?" My therapist had recognized a teachable moment.

"Yes," I answered slowly. "I thought I was going to die."

"And now?"

"I feel normal again, and Pat is a part of the person I am today."

"And so will be the experience of your eyeglasses," she said.

While my therapist was correct for the long run, there were also some immediate benefits. Without those pesky spectacles, day-to-day logistics got easier. I could wash my face without having to remove my glasses. No more worries about them getting wet in the rain or remembering where I'd put them. No more concern about steamed-up lenses when moving from cold to warmth. The top of the nightstand became roomier. If I bumped into something, while I still had to worry about the welfare of my tender forehead, I no longer fretted that my glasses would break or my nose would take a beating.

Positive thoughts supplanted sad ones. I was proud of myself. I believed I had conquered the fear and anger that had torn away at my insides for so long. Anticlimactic? Yes. Fulfilling? Not really. However, a single act of violence against my eyeglasses would not have been satisfying either. Gratuitous violence usually isn't. Besides, rising from the deep is a lot more fun than remaining mired in the mud, contemplating what to do with a Budweiser bottle.

Approaching the Run

In the mid-1980s, I dabbled in hobby sports and sowed the seeds that would eventually lead me to my second athletic career—long distance running. I had two extended relationships and continued to pursue my doctorate, one of my other holy grails.

What Goes Up…

In 1984, soon after Pat and I divorced, I connected with a group of blind people that traveled regularly to Smugglers' Notch, Vermont, to engage in the risky business of downhill (Alpine) skiing. They introduced me to the BOLD (Blind Outdoor Leisure Development) program. In the winter, BOLD chapters around the US assist downhill skiers with disabilities to do their thing. Blind skiers receive verbal directions ("Quarter right turn," "Half left turn," "Traverse," "Get down, you're about to hit a lift stanchion!").

Skiers with reduced use of their legs utilize special apparatus such as an array consisting of a seat, main skis, and steering skis to plummet down the mountainsides. We may have been crazy thrill-seekers, but with the aid of guides that could ski backward down expert slopes if needed (and some of them did during emergency ski patrol duty), we felt safe and thoroughly enjoyed our winter experience.

BOLD provided the experts and equipment. First, guides and skiers were matched. Then paired and outfitted, teams stumble to the bunny slopes. Here, guided by our partners, we sidestepped up and down slopes and learned how to walk uphill using the herringbone technique (ski tips spread and heels close together). These exercises proved more exhausting than the actual skiing.

The guides taught us how to "snowplow" in order to make turns and regulate speed. Thus our fledgling attempts at controlled plummeting were made with ski tips pointing toward each other, heels spread, and knees screaming. Today, novice skiers are taught to keep their skis parallel and turn by shifting their weight from ski to ski. This approach is embodied in the style known as telemarking. The ability to quickly turn left and right is a crucial skill as the bulk of our control on the slopes would come from zigzagging our way down and occasionally cutting across (traversing) the steeper hills. No headlong shots for us blind guys.

Nothing brings you back to earth like the thought of leaving it. The ski lifts turned out to be an adventure every time we used them. Holding your guide's elbow and feeling his body position, you stand ready to be scooped up by a chair that rushes toward you from behind. Unable to see the chair as it rapidly approaches, half deaf from the hat that covers your ears, and claustrophobic from the goggles covering your eyes, you abruptly sit down as it hits the back of your legs. Squirming to sit upright, you gather your poles to prevent them from tangling with your guide or any of what seems to be a dozen mechanisms that comprise the lift. As if this isn't enough, you must remember to raise your ski tips so they won't stick into the ground and drag you off the chair. Then all goes quiet as you realize you are airborne.

The ride to the top is, at first, unnerving. The guide tells you not to worry. "We're only about twenty-five feet above the snow," he reassures. "Keep your skis up and parallel," he instructs. I thought I had been doing that. "Your skis are drooping, put some muscle into those legs!" I thought I was doing that too. A few trips on the lift and it becomes natural.

The ride to the top can either seem like an eternity or be much too short. It's all according to how much you dread the dismount. Leaving the lift is quite a challenge. The guide says, "Get ready," and commences a countdown. "Five, four, three, two, one, stand!" he shouts. The back of your skis contact the ground and the front of your skis hit the snow with a jolt. You stand and immediately pitch forward, fighting to keep from falling on your face. The guide orders you to glide.

Your guide announces that you will be making either a sharp left or right turn on command in order to clear the chute. "We won't know which way to turn until I see the situation," he quips. If you don't lose it, you execute the maneuver. If your body, legs, or skis fail, you either collapse in the chute or collide with a snowbank thankfully placed at the end of the chute for such emergencies. Although you end up looking stupid as you shake snow from places you didn't know you had places, at least you're alive.

Once, when my guide gave me a staccato countdown, I didn't react quickly enough. I started to exit the chair, thought twice, and sat back down. As I hung, half out of the chair, it began to spin on its vertical axis. I hadn't known it possessed that capability. Hearing my shouts and also those of my guide's on the ground below, the lift master alertly stopped the machine before I was dragged up-range to a fate I wouldn't want to contemplate. Hauling me off my perch, the guide and lift operator comforted me, saying, "Don't worry, this happens about a hundred times every day."

Skiing down steep hills can be a turn on. My guide, a sexy young woman, called out commands from behind, alongside, and occasionally in front of me as we skied. "Quarter left, quarter right, traverse. Hard left. Now! Hard left." My reaction time must have been slow that day. My mind drifted toward fantasies of a quiet cabin, warm fire, and sharing a bottle of wine with my guide. Now, at least two commands behind and her voice finally penetrating, my attention snapped back. "Down! Down!" I heard her order. Sensing my peril, I slid into a deliberate crash.

My guide skied alongside my prostrate body. Only a second ago, her voice was shrill enough to cut metal. Now, she softly whispered, "Can you get up?" Despite the fact one of my skis, still attached to my boot, had somehow positioned itself behind my head while the other had properly detached and slid down the hill, I had to resist the temptation to feign injury. The ruse to gain her sympathy would probably have failed anyway; gorgeous young women seem to be quite aware of these tricks. All I could do was plaintively answer, "Yes, I'm okay."

As I smiled up at her, she bent to help me get to my feet. Half out of genuine need and half out of naughtiness, I leaned against her for support and asked, "Can we go home now?"

There were many occasions when I panicked because my speed had increased beyond my tolerance threshold. Noticing this, and instead of risking an accident, guides would tell me to go into a controlled crash. This was something we trained for. Skidding sideways on the edges of my skis, I would slide to the snow and pray my body would stop before hitting a tree or the edge of an embankment.

Getting up is no picnic. If a crash occurs on a slope, one should stand perpendicular to it, push off its uphill side, and let gravity pull him to an upright position. Doing this with skis still attached to your boots and poles in your hands is quite strenuous. After several falls, one begins to get tired of both the energy it requires to get to one's feet and the humiliation. Falls are usually caused by loss of balance either due to weight being shifted too far back on the skis or hitting an ice patch and sliding out of control.

With three winters and seven trips to Smuggler's Notch under my belt, my skills developed to the point where the trainers felt I could handle the intermediate slopes, this despite the fact that I fell down exiting the ski lifts about half the time. The main differences between the beginner slopes and the intermediate ones are the steepness of the hills and the sharpness of some of the turns. To handle the more difficult slopes, the blind skier needs to be in superb shape and have strong, quick reflexes. It also helps to have steady nerves, a well-developed need for speed, and a love of the downward plummet. Personally, I loved speed, but I had no stomach for rapid descent toward things I couldn't see. After trying a few runs, picking myself up off the snow more than I cared to, I asked my guide to set me back a grade. My leg muscles weren't in good-enough shape to handle the continual stress of making the extra turns required to traverse the hills,—left, right, left, right, over and over. I happily returned to the comfort of the still-challenging, but more benign, advanced-beginner slopes.

To be sure, many blind skiers have mastered the advanced slopes. The issue is one of skill, strength, and nerve, not blindness. Hitting a plateau gives one pause. He assesses his abilities as well as his toughness. Was I not as dedicated as I could be? Was I a coward? Such circumspection leads to a deeper if not more sober appreciation of one's own athletic ability.

Deflated but not defeated, I began to put things into perspective. I contemplated what an idealized image of myself as an athlete might look like. I selectively remembered my best wrestling matches. Would I ever find another sport like that—a sport for which I had innate talent?

Perhaps, I thought, the trick is not to worry about becoming a super achiever but to enjoy the endeavor for its own sake. I decided that the greater cache lay in diversification.

Gliding Along

Cross-country (Nordic) skiing was easier to learn. In the early 1980s, I still had enough vision to see what was directly in front of me. With a little guidance and verbal direction on tricky downhill turns, I managed to get through the trails of various parks north of New York City. Years later, I accepted an invitation from the United States Association of Blind Athletes (USABA) to train for their team with an outside chance of making the Paralympics. By then, most of my eyesight had faded. Any special techniques they would teach me would have to work without use of compensatory residual vision.

I flew to Winter Park, Colorado, anticipating with glee the opportunity to learn from the masters. We trained at above ten thousand feet. In the classroom, I learned about the effect of altitude on breathing, efficiency of oxygen uptake, proper nutrition, and techniques that promote fitness. Out on the mountainside, they taught me to ski.

I discovered that a great boon to blind cross-country skiers is the convention of cutting tracks in the snow. Unlike backcountry skiing where the snow is usually virginal, cross-country trails prepared in advance can be a joy to traverse. Park staff use snowmobiles equipped with track-making skids to drive over the trails and cut the tracks. Before this machinery was available, intrepid lead skiers simply traveled the trails and cut the tracks as they went along. Follow-up skiers, placing their skis in the same tracks, deepened the tracks and packed them down.

For we who cannot see, skiing in premade tracks provides invaluable guidance. When you don't have to worry about drifting too far left or right on a trail, when you save huge amounts of energy by keeping your skis out of thick snow, and when making simple turns as the trail curves around terrain and trees is a nonevent, your experience becomes quite pleasant. On curvy downhills, placing one ski outside a track and leaving the other inside one enables a skier to follow the curve with little guidance from a sighted partner. The outside ski can be angled into a half snowplow, or its edge can be dug into the snow to assist the turn. On more severe hills, I found it effective to take both skis out of the tracks, use a snowplow to slow my speed, and place more weight on the outside ski to effectively negotiate the turns.

As it turned out, a few of our sighted instructors were contenders for spots on the US Olympic team. I also met several highly talented blind athletes who probably went on to the Paralympics. Despite the fact I was no match for them on the snow, we became friends. Reminiscent of the time in college when I refused an interview with the *New York Times* because I didn't feel I was a good-enough wrestler to warrant the attention of the public, I headed home with a renewed appreciation for the difference between a blind person engaging in athletics and great athletes who happened to be blind. A Nordic dabbler at best, I had gone to Winter Park to try the sport on for size. Living, training, and socializing with excellent athletes and instructors not only filled me with appreciation for their skill and dedication but taught me that my true desire did not really lie in that level of competition.

My cross-country skiing career extended into the 2000s when I lived in Northern California. The Sierra Regional Ski for Light program is part of an international effort to bring blind people of all skill levels to the cross-country tracks, trails, and hills. I was fortunate to have some good training from dedicated guides and lots of camaraderie on the few weekend trips I made with Sierra Ski for Light. Even more exciting, although I never made it there, are the weeklong national gatherings in various select locations held each year.

Superman, Supernova

Excelling at work, I received a promotion soon after Pat and I broke up. They made me a supervisor. The promotion was fortuitous. I needed the money. Graduate school and increased cost of living were eating up my paycheck. Making ends meet was harder than when Pat and I had shared expenses.

In 1985, I met a very nice lady in a personality theory class at NYU. She was auditing; for me, it was a requirement. We got to know each other walking to the A train after class—she, heading toward Inwood, I toward Riverdale with a switch en route to the number 1 IRT. We dated for the next two years.

Joan worked as a writer for a syndicated Christian television program and had been a reporter years earlier. She audited the class out of general interest and perhaps to explore budding aspirations to become a social worker, an occupation she would enter years later. We went on a few dates and then, for reasons that were probably significant, spent a few weeks out of touch. Throughout our relationship, we would have a few such hiatuses. I don't recall who got in touch with whom, but after talking by phone, we decided to go on another date. Since no one told us to stop, we kept on dating.

Joan was a more reserved person than me. Still, she captured my interest. She was aware of almost everything there was to know about the social issues of our times; I was lucky if I managed to listen to news radio for an hour or so per day. She read numerous magazines and newspapers; I read perhaps one book a month. Her interests were eclectic; I dabbled mostly in science and historical fiction. Her family was warm and welcomed me into their homes. We spent the Christmas of 1986 partly with them and partly with my family.

Meanwhile, I continued to take courses at NYU. By 1986, I had completed most of my coursework and passed my comprehensive exams. That year, Bob, who had turned seventy-five, sold me his car.

Bob owned a 1974 Chevy Nova that he no longer felt safe driving in the city. He sold it to me for $500, complete with a floor shifter that slipped when engaging first gear on uphills. I had the shifter fixed twice. The first time, the mechanic at a service station near where I lived installed it backward. Instead of shifting to the lower left for first gear, suddenly, the lower left became reverse. Two coworkers and I nearly crashed the car trying to exit the lot. "Do you want to bring it back to that guy?" they asked. "No," I said through gritted teeth. "Drive me to Joan's, and we'll compensate until I can figure out what to do."

I had the job done the right way at a brand-name transmission center. Shortly thereafter, written report from the center in hand, I took the service station to small-claims court.

Joan and I trudged to the Bronx County courthouse. I secretly hoped the gas station owner would not show up. But there he sat when we arrived. We told our stories to the judge.

The service station owner claimed his mechanic had done the job correctly. Referring to me, the owner speculated, "He must have had the job done over for some reason." The judge was not fooled. He awarded me a settlement, and the service station paid up.

"Whew!" I exulted. "I'm sure glad I didn't have to call the sheriff's office to enforce the settlement. It would have been a zoo."

"I'm glad too," Joan agreed. "Had he put up a fight, we wouldn't be able to walk past his station on the way to the subway without worrying."

Next came the task of insuring the car. I dreaded this part, assuming that I'd be turned down as soon as I walked in the door, white cane in hand. When I was nineteen, my father asked his life insurance salesman to come to the house to sell me a plan. The salesman was happy to do so, but at a higher premium than usual. "Because of your poor eyesight," he stated, "you are a poor risk." Upset by what felt like blatant discrimination, I didn't have sufficient wind in my sails to argue with him. I accepted the terms he offered and resented it for years thereafter. Here I was again, facing the prospect of rejection.

It turned out to be easier than I thought. All the agent did was ask me for the ownership papers, a copy of Joan's driver's license, and my assurance that I wouldn't drive the car myself. Thankfully, he complied with the law and not his own preconceptions. All I had to do was list Joan as my "designated driver." On the advice of the agent, I insured the car only for liability. "It's not worth insuring the car for collision," he assured me. "It wouldn't take more than a thousand dollars' worth of damage to total it."

To prove times do change, about ten years later, in the midnineties, I managed to buy additional life insurance without prejudice and at the same rate as anyone else my age.

Joan kept the car near her apartment building. From her days driving around Westchester County as a reporter, she already knew how to drive a stick shift. Had she needed, I could have taught her, learning to drive stick years ago in an old Volkswagen Beetle that my teenage friends and I had converted into a dune buggy to ride around in open fields. Moreover, we hadn't been going out long enough for the husband-and-wife syndrome to have set in. In this scenario, domestic discord rises dramatically as each spouse denigrates the other's (usually gender-related) incapacities to near-destructive levels. Driver's education schools reap the benefits.

Although the Nova turned out to be a bear, it did give us wheels. We used it to drive in the Metropolitan area, shopping and visiting our respective families. Once we drove it all the way to Bar Harbor, Maine and, via a ferry, to Nova Scotia. Driving around the island on the Evangeline Trail, visiting Sydney, Halifax, Yarmouth, and the Kejimkujik National Park was a wonderful formula for a vacation.

One August day, Joan and I took the Nova to my parents, picked up the canoe, and strapped it to the top of the car. We traveled to Forked Lake in the Adirondacks for a few days of paddling and camping. Pat and I had made this trip a few times, and after she and I split up, I managed to drag my brother Lenny up there, but only once. The lake supported dozens of state-run campsites. The only way to get to them was to load up a canoe and paddle for a half hour or so.

We pitched our tent, gathered firewood to use in the prefabricated stone fireplace provided with all campsites, and slung a tarp with ropes thrown over branches. It was at this point I decided to practice jumping rope with a spare piece. I leaped up, came down, and crumbled to the ground. My back had gone into a giant spasm. The pain was so great I was unable to straighten up. It had been a while since my back had done this. "The last time I felt this bad," I told Joan, "was in college, when I resumed wrestling after laying off for two years."

I spent the next three days bent over like a twisted pretzel. It was while we sat on the shore—I, nursing my back, and she, gazing out onto the lake—that the bear appeared.

The campsites at Forked Lake had been experiencing increased encroachment for a few years. Naturalists complained that the bears had been made too tame by campers leaving food within their reach, and now the campers were paying the price. I became so nervous about encountering one that every twig that cracked, every leaf that fell sounded like a bear. I was imbued in bear paranoia. The appearance of the real thing was, of course, anticlimactic.

"It's a bear!" Joan exclaimed. Even though I still had a bit of usable vision, I didn't try to look. I froze in place, remained seated, and listened.

The bear didn't react to Joan's exclamation. Instead, he rummaged around our food bags, which we had out on a picnic table, crunched into a can of Chunky soup, and then, unceremoniously, walked away. Joan and I packed up, loaded the canoe, and left Forked Lake forever.

Returning to the city, we resumed a safer life. A successful professional, a car owner, and once again in the bosom of a satisfying relationship, I was ready for my next big step.

Out of Town

Pronounced fit by the professors at NYU to take a one-year required internship, and after several rejections, I was accepted at the VA Medical Center in Montrose, a psychiatric facility located in Westchester County, north of New York City. I felt fortunate to land a spot at this particular hospital as its clinical orientation and openness to various schools of psychological thought would hone my skills. In my year there, I learned a lot about mental illness, community mental health, clinical assessment, substance abuse, and Vietnam War–related posttraumatic stress disorder. I also learned that all of us have some tendency toward addictive behavior or even occasional psychotic thinking.

Most of us are fortunate in that we have developed a solid grounding in reality and an effective set of defense mechanisms. We've been lucky to have lived in a supportive and nontraumatic environment. The absence of abnormal brain chemistry also helps. However, until you've worked in a psychiatric setting, the notion of normalcy is just so many words. Seeing the extremes of mental, emotional, and behavioral functioning puts the mundane actions of most people we know into calm perspective.

I began my internship in September of 1986. On leave from my job with only a $10,000 stipend from the VA for the yearlong commitment, I had to curtail my activities and tapped my savings. The internship challenged me in new ways. I used every adaptive skill I possessed, including all my remaining vision, to facilitate my acclimation. Then I invented new techniques so I could take full advantage of the variety of experiences offered by the hospital, psychologists, psychiatrists, nurses, and patients.

To speed my learning of the hospital complex, Joan and I obtained a map of the campus. Her verbal descriptions, supplemented by her tracing my hands over the map, were sufficient for me to construct a tactual rendition of the grounds.

My "braille map" consisted of horizontal and vertical lines fashioned into squares that represented each building. I placed a braille number within each square exactly like the printed map and created a legend. Dashed lines symbolized roads or places where buildings were interconnected.

Rendering the map of the campus in my own hand enabled me to learn it faster than any of the five interns in my cohort. Essentially, the sprawling campus was composed of two concentric circles of buildings. Buildings on the inner ring were connected on the surface by glass-enclosed hallways. During inclement weather, one could travel between many of the buildings using underground tunnels. Roadways encircling the campus led to the outer buildings. Getting to a few of them required hoofing it as much as the length of a football field. Griping all the while, my fellow interns and I begrudgingly agreed that running back and forth across the complex from assignment to assignment had noticeably improved our cardiovascular efficiency.

After a week of general orientation, I reported to my first rotation, the Vietnam Veterans' posttraumatic stress unit. The building was situated on one of the outer circles. When I arrived at her office, my supervisor happily called the assistant director and told him I had made it safely and on time. "We certainly are glad to have you here," she said. "We'll be keeping you busy."

"That's fine with me," I answered confidently. "What type of treatment do you provide here?"

My supervisor explained that the unit might be one of the toughest rotations in the hospital. She seemed to be hinting that the assignment was too difficult as a first rotation. Seeing a worried look spread across my face, she quickly reassured me, "Don't worry. I've reviewed your file, and because you have so much professional experience, I think you will do well here."

She was right about the difficulty level. Unlike patients in the "back wards," the guys in the PTSD unit seemed very normal. They were close to my own age, and except for their stress disorder and (typically) a history of substance abuse, it was impossible not to identify with them. In fact, I found myself both fearing them and yet feeling affection for them at the same time.

In 1971, when I reached my eighteenth birthday, I paid a mandatory visit to my local draft board. By then, the military had already instituted a lottery that selected nineteen-year-olds for service. If you were unlucky enough to be drafted and even more unlucky to be sent to Vietnam, the odds were that you would land in country some time during your nineteenth year. In fact, that was the average age of a foot soldier in Vietnam. If you survived your mandatory one-year stint, you were kicked back into the world, a ragged twenty-year-old, with little debriefing and even less fanfare.

When I came upon the scene, the men (and a few women) in the unit were in their late thirties. The treatment regimen included individual counseling, various other activities, and a structured form of group therapy that required the vets to tell their stories from birth to the present. The most important part of the therapy was the reliving of the traumatic events in their Vietnam experience.

Every afternoon, after listening to the veterans' stories, I sat alone in my office, stunned by what I had just heard. Visions of grenades thrown inside hooches, explosions, and screams of women and children reverberated in my head. Images of GIs with their faces blown off or legs and testicles mangled by Bouncing Betties (a dastardly type of land mine) made me cringe.

Some of the more disturbing stories I heard were those that sprung from various encounters the men had with Vietnamese women. Occasionally, things went terribly wrong, resulting in each doing horrific violence to the other. By far, the most gut-wrenching stories were of men encountering fellow GIs who had been captured, obviously tortured, and then skewered on sharp bamboo poles, their ears and other parts cut off, and left to die.

The images left me sick and exhausted. I'd debrief with my supervisor, go home, try to fight off the temptation to cry, and take a short nap before I could muster the strength to fix dinner.

My supervisor offered, "You will feel your own trauma welling up from inside as you listen to the Veterans' stories."

"Yes," I agreed. "My own trauma comes from loss of eyesight and some of the beatings I took as a wrestler."

"You can use these experiences to empathize with the Veterans and also as part of your own healing process," my supervisor said. "That process never ends."

After a few weeks, the stories stopped bothering me. A new dynamic took over—a sadistic desire to hear even more of them. Thankfully, my supervisor anticipated this part of my development and counseled me. "You must take the desire to absorb their trauma and use it to understand what can happen to all of us if placed into the wrong environment. In this way, you will be able to help the vets process through what happened to them."

Meanwhile, I was becoming more acutely aware of my own trauma. The supervisors had warned us that much like medical students becoming hypervigilant about physical symptoms, psychology interns were prone to hyperintrospection. If we weren't careful, they told us, we might begin to think we were closet examples of everything that might be found in an abnormal psychology textbook. "The next thing you know," one of the younger psychologists chuckled, "You will be approaching the psychiatry staff requesting Xanax."

In a clinical environment, introspection is not only a compulsion, it's a requirement. The interns fell right into line. We met with each other to discuss our experiences. Once a week, we gathered for group supervision with a member of the staff. In effect, this was group therapy. We even got on each other's nerves. I tended to talk a great deal while one of the women in my peer group never said a word. I was chastised for monopolizing, she for resisting.

"You've heard the old therapist's joke," our group leader said one day. "If your client is early for the session, he's anxious. If he's late, he's resistant. And"—he snickered—"if he's on time, he's obsessive-compulsive."

Piled on top were our individual supervisory sessions. Not only did these sessions cover the treatment and clinical aspects of our cases, they (necessarily) also focused on our reactions to what we heard. Combining my own weekly therapy sessions with all this other analysis left me raw.

My therapist and supervisor both said essentially the same thing. "You will have to get on top of your own trauma so you can use it to benefit both yourself and the vets. If you can't get on top of it, you will do neither."

At one point in the yearlong sojourn, I rotated to a substance-abuse rehabilitation unit. While there, I decided I'd become a sex addict. "Did you know there is something called sex anonymous?" I asked one of the interns. "Yes," he answered. "I signed up last rotation."

When I rotated to a psychiatric rehabilitation unit, I became convinced I was paranoid. "I think not being able to see well and perhaps the slow diminution of vision over so many years is nothing to sneeze at," I told my therapist. "It's making me feel like I've been waiting for something to happen to me since the day I was born."

"Well," she prodded, "has anything happened?"

"No," I said. "Not unless you call going slowly blind and the breakup of my marriage *nothing*."

Over time, I had come to realize that throughout my life, each time I could no longer see something I was once able to see, I suffered what my therapist called another "serial loss."

"By themselves, these losses might cause some depression," my therapist said. "But not necessarily paranoia. Don't worry about it," she assured. "I see no evidence that you are paranoid."

"What about my father's punishing attitude toward me?" I asked. "Wouldn't that make me paranoid?"

"That is something we can explore further," she admitted. "Remember," she added, "paranoia generally has little basis in observable reality. Your feelings are more like those experienced by some of the veterans you've told me about. Remember the symptom of hyper vigilance?"

"Yes," I answered. "The vets have been through trauma. Now, they keep looking over their shoulder, waiting for something else to happen."

Referring me back to my experiences in the PTSD unit, she asked, "Do you feel traumatized?"

"I think I do," I answered. "My father wasn't always the gentlest man. He frightened me. Sometimes, he administered corporal punishment a bit too vigorously. Perhaps, some of those losses on the wrestling mat were the result of my being afraid to get beaten up. Other losses might have been so overwhelming that I absorbed them as if I'd actually been attacked."

"Those are good insights," my therapist agreed. "This is something I think we can look into," she said. "However, I think you've done a marvelous job in overcoming a great deal already. You have a great deal of resiliency and lots of energy."

Another major challenge during my internship was conducting clinical testing. On at least one occasion during the process of applying for internship slots, the interviewer asked, "How will you administer the Rorschach and the TAT, the WAIS and the HTP?" These tests were key parts of a standard clinical test battery. The Rorschach and TAT (Thematic Apperception Test) required the clinician to show the client picture cards. The Rorschach inkblots were of nothing in particular—just lots of black, white, gray, and colorful shapes. The TAT cards had photos of real images, usually of people engaged in ambiguous situations. Clients are asked to tell what they see, and interpretations are made on the content, timing, and mood of their responses.

The Wechsler Adult Intelligence Scales (WAIS) is a series of subtests. Some require the examiner to read questions aloud and record the answer and how long it takes for the response. For the first task, I tape-recorded the questions in my own voice and played them aloud to the patients. I used a second tape recorder, left in "record" mode throughout the session, to record their answers. Using a standard stopwatch, I simply asked the patients to read what the watch said and recorded the data. Today, I would use an electronic device that can be handled by a blind person independently. Other subtests required the examiner to set up blocks or paper-and-pencil tasks and observe the client in action. After becoming thoroughly familiar with the process, I felt I always knew what was going on. In the case, say, of the block design test, I could touch the blocks that I had marked on each side with braille symbols and tell how the examinee had arranged them.

The HTP (house-tree-person test) asks clients to draw a picture of these three items. Via the drawings, interpretations can be made on both the person's mental and neuropsychological functioning. For example, if the house is drawn out of scale or off to one side of the page, the examiner queries the individual and then considers in his report various hypotheses shown actuarially to correlate with the behavior. To accomplish these tasks, I took the drawings to a trained reader to make sure I fully understood what had been drawn and then made my hypotheses. Notes in hand, I reinterviewed the examinees the following week to make sure I'd covered all bases. Then I'd write my report.

Psychologists do not interpret these tests in isolation. They are always done in combination with a clinical interview. Referrals come from case managers who work with the clients and who feel the information gleaned from testing will help the treatment process move along. By the time psychologists receive referrals for testing, a great deal is already known about the examinee, and they have in hand the specific questions the case manager had in mind when making the referral.

The same questions about how I would do testing were posed by all my internship interviewers. My answers were often met with skepticism ("I took a course in testing." "I place braille marks on the back of the Rorschach and TAT cards and make notes on each picture." "I tape-record the answers and analyze them later." "A sighted reader sits with me.").

"That sounds good in theory," the internship interviewer answered. "I'm not convinced you aren't corrupting the interpretation with all those adaptations. The injection of another person into the interpretation process makes it even more problematic for me." It was no surprise when I wasn't accepted at several of the internship sites at which I interviewed.

Happily, the folks at Montrose were much more open-minded. They let me try out my techniques and provided close supervision. Occasionally, one of my supervisors might disagree with how I went about administering a particular test, and together, we would finetune the process. In the end, they wrote in my evaluation summary that my batteries were well administered and of satisfactory quality.

In the spring of my internship year, Joan and I began to pull apart. Joan seemed to have grown ambivalent about our relationship. I had some thoughts about why. Perhaps I was too high-strung for her. Perhaps I had begun to press, and she didn't want to make the long-term commitment I may have been looking for. We disagreed about how much time we should spend together. Entire weekends went by without a call. I grew frustrated and lonely. The overwhelming number of new and demanding things I had to deal with at the internship may have caused me to search for a security blanket. Joan was no longer providing it. Finally, after spending the Memorial Day weekend of 1987 alone, I called Joan to ask her if she wanted to end our relationship. She reluctantly agreed.

While the dissolution of our relationship was painful for both of us, there was still one thing that bound us together. We needed to dispose of the Nova. Joan continued to mind the car while I searched for a way to get rid of it. A few months later, having returned to work, I donated it to a charity in Harlem. Unfortunate as it was to have broken up, Joan, I'm sure, was relieved to be rid of the responsibility for moving the jalopy from one side of the street to the other.

At the end of August, having learned a great deal about substance abuse, psychiatric rehabilitation, and, most relevant I thought to my personal experiences, the effects of trauma, I successfully completed my internship. Full of clinical knowledge of the symptoms of personality and mental disorders, replete with knowledge of psychotropic medications and the intricacies of the clinical testing and assessment process, I returned to work convinced I would be a better supervisor and, someday, a real doctor.

In first-year doctoral seminar, our professor told us that part of our motivation for entering the program was the power that came with a PhD. At that time, I thought little of his pronouncement. However, in my internship, when the first veteran addressed me as "Doc," all doubt vanished. I loved it. Later, I found out that military men and women tend to call anyone, including corpsmen and medics, "Doc." It didn't matter. I was smitten.

While we were on internship, NYU required us to return to campus for monthly meetings. The policy had been implemented so students wouldn't be out of touch with the faculty for excessively long stretches. We discussed our experiences, and the professors gave us advice on how to get the most out of the training opportunity. They encouraged us to take full advantage of the clinical exposure we received and commence serious research into topics for our doctoral dissertations. They rightly told us that we might never have the chance to be around so many nurturing professional psychologists as while in our internships. "Once you go to work, you will be expected to hold your own," they said. "Now, they expect you to ask lots of questions. Do not forget to do so."

I returned to school with a newfound interest: cognitive behaviorism. Spawned directly from my exposure to a few behavioral psychologists at the VA, I eventually narrowed my interests to "self-efficacy theory" and a direction for my dissertation.

Self-efficacy theory is part of a greater cluster of cognitive-behavioral theories called "expectancy theory." Seligman's concept of "learned helplessness," to which I gravitated as an explanation for some of my wrestling "head-problems," can be explained through expectancy theory.

Simply put, "self-efficacy theory" predicts that you will attempt and persist at doing things for which you believe (expect) you have a chance at mastery and, therefore, success. You may say, "It sounds simple." Well, that's how good theories should sound. Contrary to the pop psychology of the mid-'80s, self-efficacy theory is more a predictor of behavior change than a theory of global personality. It concerns itself with how people's thoughts lead to what they do, all the while understanding that people's thoughts derive from prior learning and the emotional connection they make to what they have learned.

Gearing up to pursue my dissertation, in September, I reported to the NYU Disabled Students' Center to obtain readers and library assistants. To say the least, dissertation research is reading-intensive, and I needed all the help I could get to find articles and books at the library and have them recorded onto cassette tapes. The intern assigned to help me at the center was an attractive student in the rehabilitation counseling master's degree program.

About my age, Barbara was a stroke survivor, with residual weakness on her right side, quite bubbly, and immediately interested in me as more than just her client. She discharged her counseling duties quite well, finding me two readers to help me do my library research. That out of the way, she asked me to dinner. We dated for about a year.

Barbara had stepped down from her position as vice president of her family's bookstore to pursue her professional interest in working with people with disabilities. She had originally trained to be a teacher, suffering a paralyzing stroke at age twenty-one, only a month before starting her first job in an elementary school in Upstate New York, not far from Ithaca College where she'd just graduated. She spent years in rehabilitation, regaining almost full use of her body. She even wrote a book about her foray into the depths of disability and how she eventually returned to Ithaca. She went on to become a national advocate for head-injury services and now runs a Yoga school in Tampa with her husband.

Splashdown

My brothers and I had always enjoyed the water. As early as the late 1970s, we joined forces to purchase small boats in which to tool about the Hudson River and surrounding waterways. As the years went on, we graduated to larger runabouts that enabled us to patrol the Long Island Sound, New York Harbor, and parts of the East Coast inland waterway. We even traveled north to Lake Champlain via a connecting canal, replete with locks barely large enough to hold the barges that still carry materials from the Hudson into the lake. We also purchased waterskiing equipment.

I'd never even touched a water ski until the day I donned a life vest and sat alone in the Hudson, skis waving in the breeze as I tried to point them toward the sky. Lenny piloted the boat. Barbara and my youngest brother, Joe, stood astern, Joe laughing in anticipation of what was about to transpire and Barbara terrified. Waving tentatively in the direction of the boat, I waited for it to jerk me to my feet.

Lenny gunned the twin engines on the twenty-four-foot Sea Ray, and it lunged forward. The force that pulled me to my feet put more pressure on my arms than I'd ever felt—even while under attack from brutishly strong adversaries on the wrestling mats. I rose to an upright position and immediately fell forward onto my face.

The skis, as they are supposed to do, flew off my feet. I submerged and then, with the help of a buoyancy vest, popped to the surface. I paddled around while Lenny turned the boat. Returning to my position in the water, he coached me while Joe reached over and rounded up my skis. Positioning the boat for another try, he called out, "This time, keep your knees and elbows bent, your head up, and your back straight."

Embarrassed and wondering if I would ever be able to remain standing on the long thin boards, I braced for another jolt. A few attempts later, I managed to stand. Now the trick was to stay on my feet for more than one or two minutes.

It was hard to predict when I would hit a swell and be thrown off balance. Even scarier, I didn't want to drift too far to either side of the propeller streams. That would mean I was outside the zone that the boat had just plowed through and vulnerable to colliding with debris, buoys, other boats, or skiers also drifting outside their safe zones.

I had only the sound of the boat engine and the dual wakes roiling behind the propellers to guide me. At that time, I still had the ability to see the white foamy water streaming toward me from the rear of the boat like contrails from jet engines. Then it happened.

I water-skied for the last time on the Fourth of July, 1988. The accident was spectacular. While zipping along at an ungodly speed, I was caught by surprise and hit a ripple. This shouldn't have been a surprise as I really couldn't see the subtleties (wavelets, ripples, small eddies, and vortices) presented by the swirling water in front of me. I began to pitch forward.

Fighting to stay upright, I hung on to the ski bar a split second too long. With the sleek gracefulness and destructive force of a harpoon, I speared the water, face-first. My body immediately submerged. The ski bar ran up my left arm and, as my body decelerated, was ripped forward and away from me by the still-speeding boat. I tumbled head over heels underwater and, thanks to the mandatory life vest, popped to the surface and rolled to my back. It was only then that I felt the intense pain envelope my left arm.

Lenny steered the boat around to pick me up. "Are you okay?" he called. Writhing in pain, I managed to squeeze out, "No, I hurt my arm." Then I leaned back and fought to keep from fainting from the pain and nausea.

A river ambulance took me from our boat to the shore. Barbara cradled me on her lap. Ashore, a land ambulance met us and brought me to the nearest hospital. Dressed only in a bathing suit and chilling down fast, I was wheeled into the emergency room and directly to the check-in desk. "Do you have any insurance?" the young woman behind the window asked.

"Do I look like I have anything at all?" I replied angrily. Barbara bade me to calm down.

Several X-rays later and growing nauseous from shock and lowered body temperature, I insisted on lying down and being covered by a blanket, immediately feeling better. The news that I hadn't broken any bones further raised my spirits.

The article in the *Rockland Journal News* listed me as one of the casualties of the July Fourth weekend under the category of river events. I suffered severe bruising, a great deal of swelling, a lot of humiliation, and enough respect for the sport to put it on the shelf. In its place, I took up long-distance running.

Achilles and the Marathon

Late in 1988, at the urging of my friend Elaine, I joined the Achilles Track Club. She had attempted to get me to join on two previous occasions, but I balked. "I'm not a runner," I complained. Elaine persisted. It would do me good, she said, and there would be no pressure. "Just go to a practice," she urged. "You don't have to compete. Just do whatever you find comfortable."

I'd been feeling sluggish. I had gained weight in the year since I completed my clinical internship. Working steadily through my courses since 1981, by the fall of 1986, I had completed nearly all of them. Passing my qualifying exams permitted me to do two critical things: pursue an internship and begin writing my dissertation.

My internship completed and back at my full-time job (thankfully, the Commission for the Blind held my position, granting me a one-year leave of absence with the promise I would give them at least three years of service upon my return), I faced the daunting task of actually writing the dissertation. No longer guided by the regimen of class requirements and the rigorous schedule of my internship program, I now needed to discipline myself to finish what I'd begun seven years earlier.

In the fall of 1988, I was single again (Barbara and I had just broken up), in a slump, and looking for a real change in my life. A year had gone by since finishing my internship and returning to my job with the state. I continued to see my therapist once a week. I worked hard on my dissertation and continued to work full-time. Not seeking a new relationship and wanting a respite even from dating, I wondered what I could do with my excess energy. Surely there must be something else. Finally, I decided to fall back on my old standby—good old-fashioned exercise.

> Restless that noble day, appeased by soft
> Drinks and tobacco, littering the grass
> While the flag snapped and brightened far aloft,
> We waited for the marathon to pass,
> We fathers and our little sons, let out
> Of school and office to be put to shame.
> Now from the street-side someone raised a shout,
> And into view the first small runners came…
> ("Running" by Richard Wilbur)

No one knows for sure, but it's a fair guess that long-distance running is as old as upright, human bipedalism. Today, certain aboriginal groups still hunt wild animals by chasing them on foot for days at a time. These hunters probably run the equivalent of a marathon a day in pursuit of their prey.

The modern marathon got its name from the famous battle between the Persians and allied Greek city-states in 490 BC. Radios and communications satellites in short supply, commanders frequently dispatched runners to convey information and pleas for help. In the famous battle, Pheidippides, an Athenian, ran to ask Sparta for help. Sparta refused, but learning that the Athenians had won anyway, Pheidippides ran to Athens to proclaim the victory. After running 150 miles in two days, he collapsed and died. It took 2,400 years for the trauma to subside, but undaunted, in 1896, marathoners reclaimed the legacy created by Pheidippides by running 26.2 miles in the first modern Olympics.

In 1897, with only fifteen men enrolled, the first Boston Marathon took to the streets. It remains one of the most elite races in the world. The winner, John McDermott, won with a time of 2:55:10. It wasn't until 1975 that Bill Rogers, who would grace the NY Marathon a year later, broke the 2:10 mark, a benchmark for elite racers to this day.

Today, more than twenty-five thousand runners participate in the Boston Marathon. The cheerleading capabilities of the Wellesley girls notwithstanding, it took seventy-five years for women to be officially allowed into the race. In 1966, running unofficially, Roberta Gibb finished in 3:21:40. A year later, signing up as K. Switzer, Katherine Switzer, literally eluding an attempt by the race director to physically drag her from the course, scrambled across the finish line in just over four hours. Today, the fastest women break the 2:20 mark in this event.

The New York City Marathon was first run in Central Park in 1970. Of the 127 starters, only 55 managed to circle the park the four times needed to complete the race. Their reward for this grueling endeavor was recycled bowling trophies. In 1976, Fred Lebow, race cofounder and future president of the New York Road Runners Club (NYRRC), took the race to the streets. Fred was one of the finishers in 1970 (the last time he would run the race until 1992).

The first New York City Marathon run outside Central Park, a five-borough extravaganza included Bill Rogers and Frank Shorter, who led 2,088 runners to the finish line. Today, more than fifty thousand (mainly serious and a few once-a-year) runners enter this most colorful race. The majority of the entrants are admitted on a first come, first served basis, a select group qualifies for automatic entry, and the remainder sweats out a lottery.

Commencing on the Verrazano Narrows Bridge, just outside Fort Wadsworth on Staten Island, and ending on the west side of Central Park near Tavern on the Green restaurant, the marathon has become a New York spectacle and a runners' icon. Male winners generally break the 2:10 mark, and women routinely crash the 2:26 barrier.

Meanwhile, in the mid-1960s, Dick Traum, a successful twenty-four-year old businessman and graduate student, awoke from surgery, after being hit by a car at a gas station, to find he had lost his right leg. Mr. Traum, a delightful raconteur with a never-say-die attitude, worked hard on his physical rehabilitation and completed a doctorate in management, industrial psychology, and human resources at NYU. Ten years later, worried about his sedentary lifestyle and growing waistline and influenced by Fred Lebow, Dick became the first person with a leg amputation to run the New York City Marathon. Having built himself up from three-minute runs while developing his "step and swing" running technique, Dick went on to run several half and full marathons.

In 1983, convinced that anyone, even those with the most serious disabilities, could engage in vigorous exercise, Dick founded the Achilles Track Club (ATC). With support from Fred Lebow and coaching provided by Bob Glover (author of several running books), Dick struggled to keep a small cadre of runners together until the concept caught on. Over the years, while membership has increased and coaches have rotated in and out, Dick stayed with the club, becoming, in his modest way, an icon for disabled runners.

The ATC provides a forum for its members to exercise, strive for good health and self-esteem, and seek competition. Free to choose their level of involvement, "Achilles," as they are affectionately known, have become a regular feature on training routes and in competitive races. Today, there are ATC chapters from Manhattan to Mongolia. Volunteers accompany Achilles members on their runs. They report for duty twice a week. When they arrive, the coach provides them with an orientation to the needs of runners with disabilities. Each runner needs a different kind of assistance. Some use wheelchairs, crutches, or prostheses; others simply require an escort. Blind runners get visual guidance and generally run at the same pace and in the same manner as sighted runners. They use a short tether to stay in touch with their sighted running partners. A few verbal signals about turns and terrain permits the pair to run like a well-oiled machine.

On race day, Achilles and their partners wear a colorful bib visible to nondisabled runners and race officials. Achilles who expect to take significantly longer than the race is scheduled to last can have an early start.

Because the NYC Marathon is one of the most "democratic" races in the country, many Achilles have entered and successfully completed it. Achilles range from those capable of completing a marathon in less than three hours to those requiring twelve hours to cross the finish line. As with most runners who enter the marathon, Achilles do not compete against each other. Their chief rivals, the clock and their own bodies, provide sufficient motivation. Most Achilles testify to the thrill of conquering the distance to achieve a personal best or the sheer exhilaration of joining the throngs, hoping to complete the race amidst the din created by thousands of delirious spectators cheering everyone across the finish line. If they need more, Dick Traum adds spice by advising his Achilles to get past "the wall" by telling them to focus on the attractive backside of a runner up ahead and keeping it in view!

Achilles and Me

> Most mornings I get away, slip out
> the door before light, set forth on the dim, gray
> road, letting my feet find a cadence
> that softly carries me on. Nobody
> is up—all alone my journey begins…
>
> —("Run Before Dawn" by William Stafford)

On a Tuesday evening in late October 1988, I reported to the Road Runners Club on Eighty-ninth Street near Fifth Avenue. Approaching what I thought was the correct building, I heard two men talking out front. It was a cool autumn evening, dusk descending upon Central Park a block to the west. My meager vision doing me little good at that moment, I bumped into one of them, or should I say, his wheelchair. I asked if I had arrived at the right place. The man said rather authoritatively that I had indeed arrived and directed me inside. "We wheelchair bums can't get into the building, so we have to wait here for Achilles to come out," he said.

Realizing that the steps to the front door prevented wheelchair users from entering the building, I had only a brief moment to think about disability rights and access to public places. This was a time when disability consumerism was building to the crescendo that would culminate in the Americans with Disabilities Act (ADA), but advocacy was not yet in my blood. I would later learn, ironically, that Dick Traum, amputee and head of the Achilles Track Club, helped Fred Lebow purchase that building on East Eighty-ninth Street—the building that enabled the NYRRC to grow exponentially and which would be its home from 1980 to the 2000s. The NYRRC now occupies a building on the West Side, just below Central Park.

Entering the club, I was immediately enveloped, like Alice through the looking glass, in a world that would change my life forever.

Inside were wall-to-wall people, talking loudly and joyously, their exuberance immediately penetrating my soul. Even though they made it nearly impossible to walk through the room or, for that matter, hear myself think, I flushed with warmth. Somehow, all the chaos seemed to organize itself around a central core—the love of running. I had found a home.

It only took a moment for me to learn another truism about New York Road Runners—to a man and woman, they are extremely accepting and helpful. With little effort, I managed to get an escort through the crowd to the rear of the first floor. There I was, pushed through a door into yet another world. I found myself in the club library, a quiet place that smelled, not like the locker room I had expected, but of leather-bound volumes. A dozen people sat or stood around a central table. A few chairs were pushed off to the sides. A desk was placed in the far-left corner. Books and bound journals filled shelves that encircled the room. Except for stacks of cardboard boxes, often filled with trophies, providing contrast to its elegance, the club library remains forever etched in my memory as a sanctuary, a safe house, and the place where my great adventure—my career as an Achilles—was launched.

I moved carefully into the room, using my cane to feel my way to an empty spot in the corner. That spot became my own. I would stow my belongings there before every practice from then on.

A fellow with a loud voice animatedly talked about his last race. He had switched from running to speed-walking to be more competitive. I later learned that speed-walking is a strange-looking hybrid between walking and running, requiring that, at all times, both feet remain in contact with the ground. I found the speaker annoyingly direct and honest. Little did I know that, a few months later, he would be my Cyrano de Bergerac.

A young woman said hello to me. It was Elaine, the friend who had recommended I try Achilles on for size. We hugged and, with her guide dog trying to separate us with his nose, told me she was proud I had taken the plunge into an Achilles practice.

Another woman entered the library. Overpowering several exuberant greetings, she called for everyone's attention. Patti Lee Parmalee, Dick Traum's trusted coach, was there to get the show on the road. She told everyone to follow her. As I moved my cane in front of me to obey, a strong hand gripped my arm. "Would you like an escort?" a friendly voice asked. I readily accepted the elbow thrust into my ribs. A thin, hard-bodied woman skillfully guided me out of the library, through the now-parting crowd, and outside.

We walked around the corner, entered Central Park at Ninetieth Street and Fifth Avenue, and gathered around our coach at a gravel-covered space just to the west of Central Park's inner drive. Patti asked us to listen up. She welcomed us to the practice and reviewed the ground rules: No one had to do more than they wished. Those training for the upcoming marathon should be planning their final twenty-mile run. Anyone not paired with a partner was to raise their hand. Everyone must warm up before starting their run. Be careful out there; it's getting dark, and we must stay on the main pathways.

I raised my hand to procure a partner. Just then, an affable voice asked if I were the newcomer Elaine had mentioned. I said yes, and Dick Traum introduced himself to me. We shook hands, and Dick assigned me a male partner. Instructing him to take me once around the reservoir, we did our stretches and walked about one hundred feet, up a few steps, and onto a cinder track. My partner assured me the track was flat and we would run one lap slowly around the reservoir—about a mile and a half, he estimated. I figured I could handle the distance, having run five and six mile routes while in college to supplement my wrestling workouts. My partner handed me the end of a fifteen-inch long rope and said, "Hold this end while I hold the other. That is how I will guide you as we run."

"Interesting," I said. Trying it while jogging in place, I noticed that the rope was flexible enough to allow our arms to swing normally. "Okay," I announced. "Let's do it!"

Once around the reservoir was all I could take! We cruised to a stop and walked to the staging area. Dick took hold of my wrist and measured my pulse. He jocularly announced that if I didn't drop dead in the next minute, I would probably become a good runner!

A week later, I returned for my second practice. In between, I could think of nothing but the thrill of that first run. As an experienced athlete, I had difficulty understanding why I had been so impressed. Later, I would come to realize that timing is everything—I was ready to transform myself once again into a dedicated athlete, something I hadn't done since my first wrestling practice so many years ago.

Standing at the staging area a few weeks later, a woman came up to me and, in a voice that immediately captured my imagination, asked if I needed a partner. I said yes, and she walked away. Then apparently having consulted with Patti, she returned, our partnership for that practice secured.

From the moment she introduced herself, I found Sharon easy to talk to. Thus when she suggested my trying something different, I readily agreed to her suggestion that we take a route that eschewed the cinder track surrounding the reservoir in favor of a four-mile road loop. "Don't worry," she assured me. "You'll be able to do it. I asked Dick, and he said you're ready."

Although I completed the route, Sharon, an experienced and fairly good runner, could see that I was fatigued and loathed to admit it. She escorted me back to the club where I gathered my belongings. Walking me to the corner, she waited with me until my crosstown bus to the West Side arrived. She said goodbye and jogged away. Now, infatuated, I had another thing to occupy my thoughts until next practice.

In the weeks that followed, I gradually increased my mileage and joined Achilles for Saturday practices. Introducing myself to the leader of the NYRRC group runs, a program instituted to protect joggers from assaults in the park, I got him to agree to provide me with a partner for yet a third day of running each week. Abdul was a tall, strong, African American man to whom I took an immediate liking. I later learned he was a Vietnam vet, a fact that further endeared him to me. Abdul gently but firmly made sure every one of his group runners was paired or otherwise grouped with companions who wanted to run the same distance as they that particular evening. He cautioned all runners to remain on designated routes and avoid places where there was no street lighting. We felt safe, if not alert to the possibilities.

I was getting stronger. Things at the club had returned to normal. With the 1988 marathon now history and the park quieter, less experienced runners returned to both the Achilles practices and the group runs. One Saturday morning, while we waited for our Achilles partners, a woman approached us, asking for the whereabouts of the group run. The vociferous speed-walker told her she had just missed them. I offered her the opportunity to run with us, and she accepted. Already experienced at training new partners, I asked Mary if she would like to run with me. She assented, and we became fast friends.

Mary was an average runner, a cyclist, and highly accomplished career woman. She had worked in the highest echelons of the social services system of a nearby state and knew Donna Shalala who became secretary of Health and Human Services and a member of Congress. As it turned out, Mary would be the key to much of the publicity I would eventually get for my running exploits.

In January of 1989, Dick Traum announced the running of the first "Achilles Handicap," a 10K race that would begin near East Seventy-second Street inside the park and end, after a crisscross route, near Tavern on the Green restaurant at about West Sixty-sixth Street. I had just run my first complete loop of Central Park (about six miles) with Sharon and, with her encouragement, signed up for the race. Sharon would not be available to run with me, but she arranged for a girlfriend, another quality runner, to be my partner. This amount of attention, I thought, had exceeded the call of duty. A month later, the speed-walker asked Sharon, right in front of me and with no prompting, if she were dating anyone. Sharon answered just loud enough for me to hear, "I don't know. I hope so." Needing no further prompting, I asked her to join me for postworkout pizza. We began dating a few weeks later.

The "Achilles handicap" started without me. Miscalculating the frequency of public transit on weekends, I arrived late to the starting area. A race official who spotted me wandering in the vicinity of the starting line escorted me directly to Dick Traum. In control as always, Dick connected me with my partner and sent us on our way. Since the start gun had fired only a minute prior to my arrival, he said, if I ran fast, I would catch up to the lead pack.

The "lead pack" was a hoard of Achilles runners who had been given a five-minute head start. This had been especially arranged for this race to give at least a few Achilles a fighting chance to cross the finish line before an elite runner caught them.

We came upon them just as the real lead pack, the elite runners approached our rear. I heard them coming before my partner did. Peeking over her shoulder, my partner's description of the mass approaching our rear conjured the image of the bulls at Pamplona—only in this case, I was about to be swarmed over and, in terms of my fragile athletic ego, gored.

Admittedly not the destructive din of charging bulls, the sound the elite runners made as they passed us—a rather annoying pitter-patter of high-RPM foot strikes on the road surface and the incongruous swishing of their wind breakers and pant legs—irked me nonetheless. Listening as they disappeared into the silence of north Central Park, I vowed I'd never allow myself to be overrun like that again. Better, I surmised, they start ahead of me where they belong than to catch and pass me.

Unfortunately, to my knowledge, the Achilles Handicap was not run again. I never found out why. Did my fellow Achilles feel the way I did about the head start? Or was the expense of running the race just too much for Dick Traum and NYRRC? Fifteen years later in 2003, Dick Traum would launch the "Hope and Possibility" five-mile run, with multiple disability and non-disabled categories.

A day later, I awakened to the first of a long series of running injuries that would be a hallmark of my career. My right foot ached so much that I decided to see a podiatrist. She examined my now-swollen extremity, announced I had a severe strain, and wrapped my foot in a soft cast. I limped around with a special shoe on my right foot for a week and then all was well.

In April 1989, I learned how if one endures, a sow's ear can be turned into a silk purse. Sharon and I decided to run a four-mile race in Central Park. These types of races can be injurious for some long-distance runners. They require the kind of fast running on hard road surfaces that demands more of your bones than they may be willing to give. I found this out the hard way. Halfway through the race, pain throbbing in my right shin, I asked Sharon if we could walk for a while. A friend saw us walking across the Seventy-second Street transverse and called out, "Are you okay?" I shrugged in her direction, put my head down, and continued to walk.

I was in so much pain that Sharon and I had to use a combination of running, jogging, and walking to complete the race. I favored my right leg so much that while attempting to jog up the east side of the park, I veered to the left and managed to trip and fall over a sidewalk curb. Sharon still considered herself a novice guide and immediately blamed herself for the mishap. I told her not to worry about it, cursed under my breath about the scraped knee that only added to my misery, and trudged on. Stepping across the finish line, we headed straight for the medical tent.

The doctor examined my throbbing shin and looked at my knee. He said with little regard for the reaction he knew would follow, "You will have to stop running for about six weeks. You've got what is most likely a stress fracture." Despite my ranting about not wishing to lose my conditioning, the doctor pronounced me out of commission. I had indeed sustained a stress fracture. "You can swim, but stay off that leg as much as possible," he told me. "In a few weeks, see your doctor and get a prescription for physical therapy."

As much as I hated to lose the conditioning I'd built up, not to mention the surprisingly real symptoms caused by withdrawal from the running high that comes with increasing mileage, the injury turned out to be a blessing in disguise. I began to swim a great deal and landed in the offices of Harriet and Dennis Surdi, my physical therapists for the next four years. There, I met Robby, a man whose simple suggestion changed my life in a delightful way.

As I sat on a therapy table, Harriet applying paste and electrodes to selected places on and around the site of my stress fracture, I asked her what might have caused the injury. Microvolts alternately trickled and then surged into my leg, giving me a tingling sensation and an occasional teeth-gritting, finger-in-the-socket jolt. The idea, Harriet explained, was to stimulate blood circulation, pain relief, and, ultimately, fast healing. "As for why this happened," she opined, "I think you may be right that your weakened right knee has something to do with it." She explained that it appeared my right leg muscles were slightly less developed than my left. "We'll have to figure out which exercises to give you to strengthen your right leg and knee."

The man lying on the adjacent table, Robby, introduced himself, assuring me that Harriet and Dennis, her husband and colleague, knew what they were doing. He told me about the master's degree program in nutrition he attended at Hunter College and his career as an orchestral and band guitarist. Several months later, he would accompany Leslie Uggams on a cruise line tour and play in an orchestra for a Broadway musical.

He regaled me with his exploits as a triathlete. An excellent all-around athlete, Robby explained that while most triathlons have open-water swims and longer distances than I might be accustomed to, he knew of a race, the New York Central Park triathlon, which he strongly believed that I could complete. Robby explained that the swim took place in a pool with lanes demarcated with ropes. "You can't get lost," he chirped. "You can use a tandem bike for the cycling, and you already know how to do the run."

I refrained from running for another month, increasing my aquatic practices at the Riverdale "Jack La Lanne's" (now 24 Hour Fitness), working my way up to half-mile swims. I imagined myself swimming the quarter-mile sprint that kicks off the triathlon in Central Park. I even practiced climbing out of the pool, grabbing my towel in one hand, my cane in the other, and walking quickly away from the pool area. I figured that, in a triathlon, a racer must be prepared to exert himself without any rest at all as soon as he leaves the pool. Thus began the mental portion of my triathlon training.

The electrodes, massage, strengthening exercises, and nature did the trick. I paid a visit to Murray Weisenfeld—in his time, the best runners' podiatrist in the city—and obtained specially fitted orthotics for my running shoes. In a month I recommenced jogging. By August, I would be ready to run the five-mile course that comprised the final leg of the triathlon. Now, all I needed was a bike.

The Tandem

My mission, and I chose to accept it, was to find a bicycle built for two that would serve multiple masters. My fantasy included a bike that not only held two people but would be light and sleek enough to serve as a racing machine and yet strong enough to withstand the rigors of New York City streets. Various friends accompanied me on scouting expeditions. After inspecting bicycles in two stores, we found a shop on the Upper East Side that had my dream bike, a Santana tandem, which I purchased in 1989 for $2,100. (Had I wanted to, I could have spent twice that much for the top-of-the-line tandems available back then.)

The Santana contained all the features a racer could want. Its frame was made of alloys that flexed nicely under the weight of two riders, especially on bumpy surfaces. With an eighteen-speed gear system, I felt confident I could handle almost any hill. Quick-release levers enabled me to adjust the seat height to accommodate any captain (the front rider) I might recruit. Slightly knobby tires were a concession to the bumpy and occasionally glass-sprinkled streets of the city.

Since I didn't know how skillful my various captains would be and since I wanted to be an active participant, I asked the mechanics to recable the gear shift levers to the rear handlebar. This enabled me to control a crucial aspect of the ride and made it imperative that the captain and I (the stoker) maintain close communications. This single adjustment enriched my cycling experience more than I could have imagined. Together, my captains and I used the eighteen-gear positions that came with my tandem, trudging up steep hills and rocketing downhill at occasionally breakneck speeds.

As an example, the captain might call, "We've got a long uphill coming." I would answer, "Let me know when to downshift." After several vigorous pedal strokes, and feeling the beginning of the hill, I would announce, "Shifting down." Then both of us momentarily reducing pedal pressure, I shifted to a lower gear. Without need for further signals, we increased pedal pressure to maintain RPMs on the uphill climb. Over the years, I have trained many captains in this choreographed maneuver.

Tandems have a short history compared to "singles." Design sketches of tandems that do not appear to have ever been built date back to 1817. The first tandem to be propelled by pedals, the "boneshaker," emerged in 1863. The pedals and cranks were attached directly to the wheel hubs; drive chains were still a thing of the future. This meant that riders needed to sit almost directly above the front and rear wheels so their legs could reach the pedals.

Early tandems with this design became notorious for being either front-heavy or rear-heavy. In 1884, the drive chain mechanism emerged as a way for the front and rear riders to be positioned away from the wheels. The chain linked leg-power delivered via the pedals to the rear wheel, enabling riders to sit more toward the middle of the bike. This change in weight distribution made tandem cycling as safe as single bike riding. By 1887, the first practical tandems hit the streets.

In 1894, pneumatic tires replaced hard rubber tires, softening the ride immensely. Two-and three-speed gearing systems now found their way onto tandems. By 1933, the derailleur and more complex gearing were added as standard design features. When I made my purchase, Santana, Burly, and Cannondale were the largest commercial manufacturers.

My experience with tandems began in the mid-1980s, when I participated in rides in New England. Arranged by the Lighthouse, an agency for the blind in New York City (now Lighthouse Guild), the trips were provided by the staff and volunteers of a "wellness" center in Frost Valley in Upstate New York. Ten or so blind stokers traveled to the center, trained on tandems, and got to know each other and their sighted captains. Gear, people, and bicycles were loaded into the center's van, and the group was driven to the beginning of the weeklong route. The first time I joined the group, we went to Maine; the second time, to Cape Cod.

We rode two hundred miles in seven days with two rest days built into the itinerary. Each evening, we unpacked fully loaded tandems, which carried tents, sleeping bags, and panniers filled with food and cookware. We camped out at night in state parks. Thank heavens for the showers!

On these rides, I met some strong European cyclists and developed sound cycling skills. Just as important, I formed a lasting and abiding respect for cycling in general and high-level cyclists in particular.

Back in New York, we trained on quiet paths in Central Park. After a while, my captains grew sufficiently confident to venture with me onto the streets. "They say," Robby once told me, "there are two kinds of riders in this city: Those who've been hit, and those who will someday be hit." This testament to the rider unfriendliness of the city streets has been echoed time and time again by skillful cyclists. Today, more bike lanes have been created and paths constructed in out of the way places, but in 1989, things were rough out there. In fact, a year or so after Robby made his declaration, he was sideswiped by a truck making a right turn at a light, sending him flying off his bike and onto the nearby sidewalk. Luckily, he suffered only minor injuries. Because my captains realized that they rode for two souls when on my tandem, they always erred on the side of caution, and I am happy to say I was never hit.

My partners and I confined ourselves to Central Park, Riverside Drive (which had a wide shoulder going all the way from the West Side to Washington Heights), and Riverdale. As our skills and conditioning improved, we tried a few organized rides, venturing into Westchester, across the George Washington Bridge and up the west side of the Hudson River, and the Five Boro Bike Tour.

Safety Patrol

In November 1989, a terrible thing happened in Central Park. A young woman was assaulted while running alone late at night. At first, the running community reflexively and correctly questioned the wisdom of her actions. Since the club had instituted organized group runs a long time ago, we asked ourselves, "Why did she feel the need to run in the park alone and in such a dangerous place as the 102nd Street cutoff at that hour?"

However, when we heard the extent of her injuries (the woman had been raped and suffered brain damage from severe head trauma), words of outrage flowed. While the police sought the perpetrator, our thoughts turned to how to prevent this horrific thing from ever happening again.

The NYRRC decided to reinstitute its "safety patrol," an organized effort by runners to help keep Central Park safe. Pairs of runners volunteered to cover any course they wished as part of their regular workouts. They wore brightly colored bibs, labeled Safety Patrol, and carried a police radio. Their job was simply to report anything untoward or suspicious they might observe while on their run. No intervention was required and in fact, it was discouraged. I decided to join the effort.

My motivations were not totally pure. I believed that given that safety patrollers were always paired, my volunteer service would bear fruit on two fronts. First, I would provide service to fellow joggers. Second, I would have a guaranteed running partner one additional day per week. (Finding partners five or so days per week had always proven difficult for me.)

I approached the safety patrol coordinator, a strong woman runner in her own right. Working for a running shoe store by day, her coordinator role was an additional duty in her busy schedule. Taking one look at my cane, she declared, "There's no way you can do this. You wouldn't be able to see what's going on out there, and you won't be able to protect either yourself or your partner." I responded by noting that my partner would, of necessity, be sighted and that we were not expected to intervene, just report. The matter went to Fred

Lebow. He ordered the coordinator to make a suitable arrangement. The solution: a safety patrol triplet. I met Adria and Kay.

Adria, with whom I stayed in touch for many years, was a strong runner who always placed high in her age/sex group in races at almost every distance. Kay was a freelance writer who was about as injury-prone as me. We stuck together for nearly three years.

We sometimes ran three abreast, but mostly we ran with one of us running "point" and two behind. Each of us took turns carrying the somewhat heavy two-way radio, tuned to the frequency of the Central Park precinct.

Once, we saw a small fire and radioed it in. Another time, an inebriated man, hassling everyone passing him on the park's inner roadway, caught our attention. Several times, we asked runners, especially women, to remove their headphones, stop listening to music, and pay attention to their surroundings.

In the end, ours was not a dangerous patrol, and we were happy it stayed that way. We experimented with different routes as we ran, had fun, and formed a great friendship.

How the Race Is Run

> Call me a joker, call me a fool
> Right at this moment I'm totally cool
> Clear as a crystal, sharp as a knife,
> I feel like I'm in the prime of my life
> Sometimes it feels like I'm going too fast,
> I don't know how long this feeling will last
> Maybe it's only tonight.
>
> —Billy Joel, "I Go to Extremes"
> (*Storm Front*, 1989)

We stand shivering, packed tightly against each other, looking toward the southern sky—and yawning. It is New Year's Eve 1991. The midnight hour approaches. Standing elbow to elbow with a group of friends—all with chattering teeth, I muse that only a few hours earlier, I'd been sitting in the warmth of the Cathedral of St. John the Divine near Columbia University, listening to the moving words of a student leader of the standoff in Tiananmen Square.

The crowd of several thousand commences a countdown. "Ten, nine, eight…" Our voices echo into the night. No, this is not Times Square. Several thousand die-hard runners, donning a variety of sweat suits, stand poise to commence the midnight run in Central Park.

"Three, two, one…" The fireworks explode over an open field. Yelling in unison, "Happy New Year," we give each other quick pecks on the cheek or slaps on the back and commence a four-mile jaunt that, for most of us, amounts to nothing more than a light jog in the frigid night air.

For all but a few elite runners invited to publicize the event, the midnight run isn't really a race; it's a fun run. Starting in front of the renowned Tavern on the Green restaurant, we jog south then east around the south part of Central Park, north to Ninetieth Street (the traditional start of most New York Road Runners' Club races), and abruptly reverse course. (Today, the midnight run utilizes a four-mile loop bounded on the south by 72nd Street and on the north by 102nd Street.)

Just prior to turning around at Ninetieth Street to loop back the way we came, we pass a table setup with small cups of champagne. I slug one down, immediately get sick to my stomach, and swear I'll never do that again. "Why can't they have the champagne at the end of the run?" I complain. (Later, the midnight run adopted non-alcoholic champagne-flavored water.) "Serves you right," Sharon quips. "You know you have a sensitive stomach."

Completing the fun run, we stride lazily past the finish line, weave our way through the crowd, and move on to a friend's apartment a few blocks away for a more relaxing party in a much warmer venue.

Most road races are not quite the delightful jog in the park provided to those who brave the midnight run. First of all, they are always run in daylight and generally follow a circular course. The 180-degree course reversal of the midnight run was unusual. Most of the time, races or practice runs traverse one or more loops and finish where they start. Central Park contains circuits measured at six miles, five miles, four miles, and even one and a half miles.

Crossing the finish line in a race is always thrilling. If he or she recognizes you, the announcer, wielding a bullhorn, blares out your name. Well-wishers clap and cheer as you cross the line and are fed into one of the finishing chutes. Your photo is snapped by an automatic camera, and before security tightened up so much, you would scurry off to find your gym bag lying with thousands of others' alongside the start area.

In those days, the club provided bagels and hot chocolate at a nearby school. This was where the awards ceremony was held. After happily rehashing the race with friends, the rest of the day is yours.

You go home basking in the glow of a race, if not well run that day, at least successfully completed. You are filled with the hope that your next race will be even better.

Intermezzo

One Sunday, after running a race in Central Park, the details of which have long since faded from memory, Sharon and I trudged to the school for warmth, food, and the usual postrace ritual. Little did I know that my smooth egress from the situation would be blocked by my old and apparently still not fully dowsed flame, Joan. I learned of her presence in the building rather abruptly. Waiting for Sharon to emerge from a restroom, I was suddenly accosted by a cheerful voice. "Tony, how are you?" Seeing my lack of recognition, the owner of the voice continued, "It's Roger, Joan's brother." I had not seen Roger since winter of 1986, well before Joan and I broke up. Staring at him in disbelief, I managed to yammer, "Roger, what are you doing here?" He told me Joan had just run the race and, after standing for an hour along the course to cheer her on, he had joined her for the food and festivities. My heart fluttered at the thought of seeing her. Then realizing Joan and Sharon might run into each other, my heart nearly stopped.

It wasn't as if I hadn't seen Joan since our breakup a few years ago. On perhaps a half-dozen occasions, I had run into her at the Road Runners' Club where she took up jogging as a pastime, not to compete, but for wholesome exercise. Her presence at a Road Runner's Club postrace event surprised me. Usually, only race competitors and their significant others attended these events. When had Joan decided to run races? For some reason, fearing the prospect of their meeting, I plotted an escape.

Alas, getting Sharon out of the building without running into Joan proved impossible. Joan, aware of my situation and curious to meet my current partner, seemed to deliberately plant herself near the only exit. The old girlfriend met the current one.

The interception took place close to the exit.

"Hi, Tony," Joan's sweet and familiar voice gently echoed. Trying to act surprised yet knowing the moment of truth had arrived, I looked around, pretending difficulty in locating the source of the greeting. "Tony, it's Joan," she said loud enough so there was no doubt not only where she was standing but who she was. "Joan," I gushed. "Roger said you were here. I just ran into him a few minutes ago. How are you?"

Fortunately, everyone was gracious. The women, surmising the situation, introduced themselves to each other and exchanged pleasantries. They diplomatically avoided any reference to me. Then as quickly as it began, Joan and Roger went one way and Sharon and I the other. Perhaps the event caused her to avoid me, or maybe it was just coincidence; but as it turned out, after the accidental meeting at the school, I didn't see Joan at group runs again. In fact, I wouldn't see her again for several years. Since we've been back in touch, I've never asked her if she did indeed avoid me, thinking it hubris on my part that our meeting had meant anything to her.

It must have meant something to me. Although I didn't appreciate it at that time, I had apparently retained more affection for her than I realized. This explains why I eventually got back in touch with Joan and why I am so proud of her subsequent accomplishments. In the intervening years, she returned to school, earned a master's degree in social work, altered her career path, and eventually became a social worker.

On the Road

There's nothing quite like road running. Road surfaces, unlike track or cross-country terrain, do not yield when the foot strikes. The body absorbs a great deal of shock. That is why the running shoes industry has flourished over the last forty years. Runners seem to be forever searching for comfortable shoes containing the latest and most effective stabilization and shock absorption systems. In the early 1990s, gel packs became all the rage. Today, the technology is far more complex, including variable inflation-deflation systems for foot cushioning.

I tried several brands before settling on my favorite. This was by no means because one brand was better than another, although I'm sure the experts can tell the difference. My hopscotch from brand to brand occurred for two reasons. First, it seemed that the running shoes companies were in a constant state of wanderlust. They couldn't seem to leave a style of shoes alone for more than a year. For example, early in my career, I found a comfortable and supportive pair of Nike Air Max. They lasted me about ten months before going flat. (The rule of thumb was a five-hundred-mile limit to even the best shoe.) With an average of about forty miles per week, by the time I got around to buying a new pair of shoes, the Air Max had changed. Suddenly, the size 9 1/2 didn't fit. They felt lumpy in places the previous pair did not. I tried on several styles of Nike and, giving up, attempted several other brands. I rediscovered my comfort level with shoes made by Asics. The model I selected held me in good stead for more than three years.

To be fair, my friends wore New Balance, Saucony, and many other brands I can no longer recall. If only I had learned what most smart runners had figured out: once you find a pair of shoes you really like, purchase two more pairs. If you purchase online, you could save lots of money when compared to shopping in running shoes stores. Make no mistake about it, the initial visit to the store and the tender loving care of a good salesperson is worth its weight in gold. The better stores train their salespeople (many of whom are runners themselves) to help you find shoes that not only feel good, but provide the proper support for your style of running.

My other reason for switching brands pertained to injuries. Runners (and I ranked among them) sustain minor injuries to the system made up of the feet, legs, hips, and backs at an amazing rate. This is so prevalent that my friends and I became adept at predicting injuries about to befall fellow runners. Watching and listening to their gait, we could perceive subtle irregularities in their foot strikes. Multiplied by thousands of strides on hard road surfaces, injuries usually arrived with the timeliness of the stork. They happened to me too.

STAND UP OR SIT OUT

Injuries led me to the podiatrist who prescribed orthotics. Among other things, this meant that my shoe size rose from 9 1/2 to 10. Orthotics are specially shaped replacements for the inner sole of a running shoe. They generally take up more space than an inner sole, thus the increase in shoe size. Of course, if you have gotten used to size 9 1/2 Nikes, it is entirely possible that after inserting the orthotic, a size 10 Asics might end up being your shoe of choice.

Running injuries come from many sources. When you end up in a podiatrist's office, the doctor seeks to find the cause in your feet. Orthotics are often the answer. They are form-fitted inserts that, when placed in your running shoe, change the way your foot strikes the ground. Forces then translate through your feet to the ankles, Achilles tendons, shins, knees, thighs and hamstrings, hips and pelvis, and lower back in a manner different than in the preorthotic configuration.

A typical orthotic is a piece of leather or plastic shaped roughly like an inside-out version of the bottom of your foot. For example, the arch in the orthotic rises to meet the arch in your foot. The idea is to get your foot to strike the ground evenly. Quality orthotics are individually form-fitted.

Back then, the podiatrist placed each of your feet into wet plaster and made individual casts. The casts were sent to a shop where the orthotics were produced. The first time you place your foot into a shoe containing an orthotic, it feels like you are standing on lumpy ground. They take getting used to, but as you wear them, the orthotics soften a bit and mold more completely to your foot. Soon, you forget they are there.

I discovered that my right foot tended to pronate (turn in) so that I landed mostly on its outer edge. Possibly due to years of compensating for a slightly weakened knee, my right leg had bowed to the point where I could pass for a cowboy. The orthotic raised the outer edge of my foot to force it to strike the ground more fully. Even distribution of the forces across the entire length and breadth of my foot, we hoped, would also reduce the kind of impact that had previously led to a stress fracture of my right shin. Although my left foot did not appear to have any problems, a left-foot orthotic was required, so when all tallies were completed, both my legs ended up the same length. Actually, to lessen the chances of my acquiring Achilles tendonitis (a malady with which I was familiar), the heels of both orthotics were thickened to reduce the amount my Achilles tendons stretched during long regimens of hill training, a wonderful way to build strength and stamina.

In the 1980s, the AAU partly divested and the Athletic Congress (TAC) assumed responsibility for governance of road racing. In fact, we purchased marathon runners' insurance from TAC. Today, most road races follow the rules of the USATF (track and field association). Road races must contain organized start and finish areas, a bona fide timekeeping system, several race officials, water stations at appropriate intervals, portable latrines, medical personnel, and more. To protect runners from automobile traffic, race routes must be approved by the communities in which they take place, police assigned, and roadways cleared. In the case of many events put on by the New York Road Runners' Club, races run in Central Park often took place on Sunday morning, when the park was closed to automobile traffic.

After my first competitive race, there was no going back. The adrenalin rush, the thrill of the crowd, the joy of being faster than some, the respect developed for those faster than you, and the challenge of finishing in a decent percentile all contributed to my addiction. Comparing my finishing time to others in my gender and age group smote me with the desire to improve. It was like the proverbial kid in the candy shop; the experience of racing makes you want more.

Packed together at the start line, my excitement and butterflies were the same as that of everyone around me. We could barely stand still waiting for the start horn to blow. Long lines at the latrines were a telling manifestation of our nervousness.

Once the race commences, it became important for me to control my enthusiasm. I wanted to break out of the start pack and run fast. This, as I would find out more than once during my running career, can lead to "leaving your race at the start line" as they say. The difference between racing and practice runs is that you will almost inevitably run faster in a race. The crowd, the presence of an official timekeeper, the controlled conditions, the special treatment given to racers on the course, and the plethora of quality runners combine to motivate you to push harder than you realize at the time. This became clear the morning after a race when I would wake up sore.

Racing is more than running a given distance. There can be strategizing and tactical maneuvering. It is good to set your race strategy beforehand and stick to it. For example, you might decide to begin a race at a slow pace and gradually increase speed as it progresses and in accordance with how you are feeling. On other occasions, if you are confident in your ability to recover from initial high-level energy expenditure, you might plot to burst out of the starting blocks and get ahead of a portion of the pack that might get in your way and slow you down. Finally, if you can do it, it is a good idea to save something for the end game. According to how you feel, it is possible to begin accelerating in, say, the last mile of the course and hold a quick pace all the way to the end. It helps if you know the hill configuration of a course, but if you have trained well and have confidence, you can run even the most difficult final mile under conditions of fatigue, it doesn't matter if you've never run the course before.

Since organized races provide mile markers along the route, runners can gauge their pace with a wristwatch. Many of my partners had specially manufactured watches with features enabling them to precisely gauge their mile-by-mile pace. They also could program their watches to help them maintain a preplanned cadence. In any case, good racers control their pace, leaving just enough for a final push at the end.

The final one hundred yards of a race should always be run at full steam. Even if you pray for death while doing so, it is important to look good approaching the finish line. A sprint at the end makes even the worst race experience look good to the spectators. It also makes you feel great to finish with a flourish. During training, one practice day per week of wind sprints and interval training (alternately running fast and slow over, say, a five-mile course) enables you to sprint hard at the end of even the worst of races.

"Marathon Man"

"Is it safe? Is it safe?" Our laughter almost prevented my Achilles guide and me from running while we intoned the famous line from the evil Zell (Lawrence Olivier) in *Marathon Man*, the Dustin Hoffman flick. It was the fall of 1989 and marathon fever was again in the air. I did not intend to run that year, having lost much training time the previous summer recovering from my stress fracture. However, with lots of triathlon training under my belt, I felt strong enough to beat the "marathon man's" time around the Central Park reservoir.

In the 1976 film, Dustin Hoffman plays a marathon wannabe, Babe Levy, who gets into all sorts of intrigue because of his older brother's spy antics. In a scene only devout Central Park runners would remember, Babe, training for an unnamed future marathon, sprints up to his girlfriend and asks her "What's the time?"

She answers, "Eleven forty seven. You're faster!"

Dustin Hoffman had just circumnavigated the Central Park reservoir on a cinder track stretching 1.58 miles. His pace, a nifty 7.27 per mile, was the time to beat.

After setting the stopwatch, my partner and I launched at full sprint. After a few hundred yards and unaccustomed to the pace, I quickly grew tired and asked if we could slow down. I wasn't used to hard sprints as I had avoided them to prevent injury ever since that fateful four-mile race the previous spring. Still, I persevered. About halfway around and realizing I may have left my race at the start, I reluctantly reduced speed again. The fact there wasn't a beautiful woman waiting at the end didn't help. Crossing the finish line, I bent over to catch my breath, convinced I had failed in my mission. My running partner informed me we had completed the loop in 11:22, a nifty 7:20 pace. I had beaten the marathon man by twenty-five seconds!

As my partner guided me to a water fountain, I took little solace in recalling that in the movie, Babe appeared fresh after his run, immediately asking his girlfriend to time him in another loop. Two days later, I still ached from the romp. More perturbing, when he made the film, Dustin Hoffman was thirty-seven years old. I had just turned thirty-six.

Returning to the library to gather my belongings after practice, I sat musing about what it would be like to run the marathon. A teammate asked me why I wasn't planning to participate, and hearing my answer, he pronounced that I was fit to "run-walk the thing." "Sign up," he encouraged, "You can walk the entire race if you wish. Just get out there and experience the course and what it's like to be on the road for such a long time." He said this would prepare me in ways I couldn't imagine. For when I was truly ready to run, he predicted, the experience would prove invaluable. I signed up.

Our coach, Patty, introduced me to Amy, a young lawyer who would be my partner for the marathon. We ran two six-mile runs to get our rhythm down and, less than two weeks after meeting each other for the first time, found ourselves at Staten Island's Fort Wadsworth and the start of the 1989 NYC Marathon.

A car service carried Sharon, Amy, and me from midtown to Staten Island. For Sharon, a marathon veteran, the "traditional" bus ride from the library at Forty-second Street had lost its allure. Amy and I, both first-timers, were so nervous, we felt grateful for the assurance of a warm limo. We arrived at Fort Wadsworth where we encountered throngs of runners, bundled in old sweat shirts and pants, milling about the staging area.

Agreeing to reunite at the home of a friend six hours later, Sharon left to join her friends. Amy and I suddenly felt alone among thousands. Contemplating our fate and feeling the chill of the brisk autumn air, we sat on the floor inside one of the giant tents set up for runners to keep warm. Our strategy was clear. I would run slowly until I felt tired and then start sequentially walking and jogging for whatever lengths of time felt comfortable.

We had arranged for Robby to join us when we arrived in Manhattan. At her insistence, Amy would remain my guide all the way to the end. "No matter what," she stated in her most lawyerly voice, "I finish the race with you." Robby's job was to provide moral support and help Amy to maneuver us around logjams of runners toward the end of the race. He would run interference by staying slightly ahead of us and asking runners to let Amy and me pass. Running attached and two abreast, we were less agile than solo runners who, to pass someone, could put on a burst of speed and quickly step around slower runners in front of them.

Trying to stay warm until race time, Amy and I alternately sipped hot chocolate and, along with scores of anxious marathoners, made frequent visits to the latrines set up on the perimeter of the staging area. Men had it easier than women, pissing in a bush or ceremoniously off the side of the Verrazano-Narrows Bridge.

Gratefully, the public address announcer finally called us out to the starting area. Following a time-worn tradition, we tossed away the sacrificial sweat pants and shirts that had kept us warm. "What do we do with them?" I asked. "Just toss them anywhere." Amy chuckled, "People are tossing sweat stuff into the trees." I didn't take the time to consider the social welfare or ecological implications. Somehow, it was enough to know that the marathon officials, having taken care of everything else to this point, would deal with the mess, hopefully by donating the clothing to homeless shelters.

Garbed in our shorts and T-shirts, we moved onto the upper deck of the bridge. I held tightly to Amy's arm to prevent us from getting separated by the swarm of runners intently surging toward the zones indicated by our race numbers. A computerized system had taken information from our race applications, assigned numbers, and specified where we should stand to start the race. Elite runners, men on one side and women on the other, stood up front. The rest of us lined up in accordance with our previous racing record. To make it fair, a correction factor programmed into the computer subtracted a preset number of minutes and seconds from the finishing time of runners starting in various zones back in the pack. The system worked remarkably well. Today, computerized chips attached to the laces of running shoes individually identify runners when they cross the start line and register their exact start time. At the finish line, the runner's race time is similarly registered and sent to the computer for processing.

We stood still for what seemed an eternity, waiting for the mayor to start the race. Several news helicopters, covering the start, hovered nearby. Runners pressed against us on all sides. Then for no apparent reason, everyone began to cheer.

Far ahead of us, a gun or horn must have sounded, but we couldn't hear it. Nonetheless, we knew that the race had started because as tightly packed as we were, the crowd compacted even more. We surged forward, imperceptibly at first. After fifteen seconds or so, we began walking. In a few seconds, we commenced slowly jogging, then a faster job, and finally, breaking free of the crowd, Amy and I began to run. A wave of nausea passed through me. Clenching my jaw in an effort to suppress it, I muttered, "I guess this is it." The long run ahead of us conjured both a sense of relief and trepidation.

It had seemed to take forever to reach the start line, but when we did, we were on a downhill slope and running freely. Impulsively, I began to run too fast. Sensing the influence of an adrenalin rush, Amy held me back, saying, "Remember the plan. We go slowly all the way."

The music of bands lining the streets of Brooklyn and loud cheers from onlookers spurred me forward. Periodically, I sensed people from the sidelines drawing close to me and wondered if the entire race would be this way. When Amy didn't flinch, I refocused and kept on jogging. When little children stepped onto the course to touch our legs and hands, Amy told me, if I tried, I might be able to touch their hands as well. I reached out twice and came up with air both times.

A flash of anger and sadness disturbed my concentration. Had the children pulled their hands away when they saw me reaching in their general direction? All they wanted, I surmised, was a quick, gentle touch. I grew concerned that my apparent groping might be intimidating them. It was unfair, I thought, that I couldn't have fun like everyone else. For some reason, at that moment, I deeply wished to touch the hand of one of the children. When I mentioned this to Amy in what I admit was a mournful tone, she told me not to worry and to focus on the twenty-five miles left in front of us. I complied, returning my thoughts to where I was and what lay ahead. However, the impression stayed with me.

I managed to jog all the way to the Queensboro Bridge, about fifteen miles into the race. The left side of the bridge deck was covered with carpets to protect our feet from the steel gratings that comprised the road surface. A lane was left open on the right side for emergency vehicles. Amy and I decided it would be judicious not to run the uphill portion of the westbound bridge, so we walked the first half of the span singing, "Feeling Groovy."

Halfway across, the bridge begins its downward slope. We recommenced our jog, making our way toward land. Following the off-ramp that sweeps a wide left turn in order to merge with First Avenue, we reached the promised land: Manhattan. Heading north, we scanned the throngs lining the avenue in search of Robby.

Thrilled for having come so far and relieved to be in familiar territory, I felt renewed confidence that I could indeed finish the run. We found additional comfort when, exactly as planned, Robby leaped onto the course from his perch on the west side of First Avenue at Sixty-fifth Street.

By the time we traversed First Avenue, crossed the Willis Avenue Bridge, and entered the Bronx, I was hurting mightily. The Van Cortlandt Track Club, with whom I had practiced, had a table alongside the course; and its captain, Dennis, pulled us over and, while massaging our legs, made us drink some water. Then abruptly, he sent us on our way. "Start running, or you'll stiffen up," he ordered.

We crossed a bridge at Third Avenue, entered Harlem, wound our way around Marcus Garvey Park, and found ourselves heading south on Fifth Avenue. The people of Harlem cheered us on. I thought this remarkable because by this time, they had seen the lead runners pass at least two hours earlier. Still, they made us feel like first-place racers.

Robby ran ahead, calling, "Blind runner!" The waves parted, and we trudged on, passing small packs of walkers, joggers, and the occasional individual running backward. I later learned that running backward provides an opportunity to rest certain aching leg muscles while allowing the runner to make some small progress along the course.

STAND UP OR SIT OUT

We entered Central Park and, as Dick and Patti had instructed, walked the long upgrade to the inner drive. (NYRRC has since eliminated this particular hill from the course.) Turning left, we grudgingly staggered into a slow job. I thought I heard Dick's voice urging us on. "No," Amy gasped, growing exhausted. "That's not him."

A mile or so later, disoriented and my right knee aching fiercely, I asked Amy where we were. Robby, running ahead of us and routinely peeking over his shoulder to monitor our status, saw Amy, barely able to speak, motioned to him. Calling out above the noise of the hundreds of people cheering from the sidelines, he encouraged us to keep running. "We're close to Seventy-second Street. You've got only two miles or so to go."

We exited the park onto Central Park South, turned right, and headed west toward the end of the race. Somewhere around Sixth Avenue, I suddenly felt wonderful. Feeling no pain, I asked Amy if she could run faster. Apparently feeling the same rush of adrenalin as I did, she agreed.

Increasing our speed, we scooted onto Central Park West and turned right into the park. A few dozen yards later, we made a final left turn and approached the finish line.

As we ran up the final hill, I recall three things: the din of the crowd in the bleachers, a sensation that I was sprinting, and total separateness from my body. All the pain and fatigue disappeared.

We passed under a banner and through the finish line. The photo shows Amy and me running in good form, bodies straight and heads held high. The clock, visible in the photo, shows us crossing the line at 4:36:43.

While Robby peeled off and jogged around the finish area, Amy and I passed through one of several rope corridors set up so race officials could tear off the lower corner of the race numbers pinned to our shirts. These contained bar codes which were fed into a processor to record our identities and race times. As soon as we emerged at the other end of the rope corridor and stood still, I felt immediately nauseated. Amy short-circuited my instinct to bend over by tugging my shirt. "Stand up and walk," she urged. "They won't let you stay here, and you'll feel better if you keep walking."

Robby draped Mylar blankets over both of us and thrust cups of water into our hands. His voice sounded distant as he said, "Drink this and keep walking. There's a table with bagels several yards from here."

I wasn't able to eat more than a bite of the bagel Robby thrust into my hand. Sharon, who completed her run a full hour before mine, strode up and gave me a hug. "You made it!" she announced, half amazed and with sincere appreciation for what I must have gone through. "Let's go get warm."

We showered and changed at a friend's apartment a few blocks from the west side of Central Park and filled our contracted stomachs with light fare. This replenished some of the nutrients drained from our bodies and helped us to recover sufficiently to walk without assistance. Later that night, at the postmarathon party held at a local hotel, Sharon and I, leaden legs and all, even managed to dance. It was the proudest day of my life.

Out of the Frying Pan

In February 1990, having just completed a 20k (12.4 mile) race in the iciness of Central Park, I joined the Van Cortlandt Track Club (VCTC) for a trip to Puerto Rico for the San Blas half marathon. Robust and confident from recent long-race successes, I felt the need for an interesting and new challenge.

We arrived to much fanfare in Coamo, a small town in the center of the island. The people greeted us as if we were rescuers coming to liberate their town from an occupation force, hailing us warmly and offering every convenience.

The race, as it turned out, capped off a week-long celebration of Coamo's patron saint (Blais, a help-giver and healer of throat ailments). More food, drink, and revelry surround and infiltrate the "Maraton San Blas" than any other race I've ever seen.

Forebodings of a bad race loomed over me. I had a cold, the temperature was above ninety degrees, and the race didn't kick off until five o'clock that afternoon. The long wait only served to tire me even more. My spirits took an additional plunge when I learned that this particular half marathon was one of the three most difficult in the world. The course included a small mountain that Dennis, our team captain, warned us could be our Waterloo if we ran too fast before reaching it. He told us about the time he hit the base of the mountain, so tired that the only way he could climb the hills was to run backward.

On race morning, the club assembled at a local branch of a hotel chain referred to by Puerto Ricans as Los Baños. One of the better runners, Mike, who had introduced himself to me at a party the night before, appeared to assign himself as our guardian angel. He told us about the race, how to remain calm, and insisted that we get together when we returned to the Bronx.

During the day, while we waited, I took a swim in the hotel pool. The locals must have noticed my form, for at lunch, they had nicknamed me the Swimmer. I should have listened to Mike and conserved energy. By start time, I was already tired.

The race commenced to great fanfare. Sharon and I ran together. The course required us to run two laps within the town of Coamo, weaving in and out of the streets until exiting into the countryside. Doing so brought little reward as a mountain loomed in front of us.

We'd only run six kilometers when, already feeling drained, I needed to walk. After a few minutes, we resumed our jog. In an attempt to psych myself up, I asked Sharon to announce only the alternate kilometer markers. Since the race was marked only in metric units, this ploy, I hoped, would make the race feel only half as long. To my already exhausted mind, ten units of distance seemed more palatable than the twenty we still actually needed to cover.

Training in New York City in February prepared us little for the ninety-degree temperatures of the Caribbean. We had planned to get in two practice runs before race day, to acclimate as well as possible. In deference to my burgeoning cold, we only ran once. In retrospect, we should have gotten into the environment a week prior to the race, but time and money prevented this.

Living in New York City provides the kind of multicultural experience that makes it easier to integrate the ways of people from around the world. Nonetheless, we had a difficult time comprehending a strange reaction we received from the spectators of Coamo. Observing me running, the onlookers noticed the rope tether linking Sharon and me together. More than once, people shouted to us in Spanish words best interpreted as referring to bondage. "Ay, los maridos!" (The married ones). "Mira! Que hacen?" (Look at them. What are they doing?) wafted to our ears from the sidelines.

Turning, I pointed at my eyes and called out, "Ciego", the Spanish word for *blind*. The effect was more powerful than I had intended. Instead of nodding comprehension, they profusely apologized and said, "Que lastima" (what a pity). After this happened twice, I stopped trying to explain why we had the rope. We simply smiled and kept on running.

Actually, we did a lot of walking. At one point, near the top of the mountain, bystanders, taking pity on our sorry souls, dumped buckets of water over our heads. Annoyed because our shoes were now filling with water, we cursed under our breath and sloshed away. Cresting the mountain, we commenced a joyful three-mile jog, downhill and toward the town and the end of our ordeal.

Surrounded by two Van Cortlandt runners who had come out to escort us as we approached, we cruised through the finish area and ground to a halt. Triumphant and nauseated, I was disheartened to learn that it had taken us well over two hours to do what should have taken less than 1:50.

Noticing my color, Dennis handed me a chunk of ginger and told me to chew on it to relieve the nausea visibly etched on my face. He did the same for his wife, who crossed the finish line right behind Sharon and me. We recovered quickly. An hour later, the entire team ate a celebratory meal and drank beer at the closing festivities.

The legacy of San Blas is my friendship with Mike, a fellow VCTC runner with whom I got acquainted in Puerto Rico. We would run and ride together for the next three years.

Mike had graduated from Fordham University with a degree in accounting. Nine years my junior, his voracious appetite for running enabled him to finish races among the top 20 percent of his age/sex group. We met, initially, at a Van Cortlandt park practice session.

Sharon accompanied me to my first Saturday morning practice. Still out of shape and recovering from the stress fracture I incurred in 1989, all I could do were the club's warm-up laps on the Van Cortlandt Park cinder track. I would sit out the rest of the workout and wait in the bleachers for the club to return from long runs on the cross-country course laid out in the park.

Sharon asked the first friendly face she saw (Mike) to jog with me. Mike is a kind man of Irish parentage. His entire family, including three sisters, lived in the Bronx. He seemed happy to slow down his pace and accompany me for a few laps, offering to run with me whenever our schedules permitted. "When you're back in shape," he offered, "the club runs one evening during the week." Feeling I could never keep up with the group, I didn't follow up on his offer.

Now, as we stood in line at the airport in San Juan preparing to board a flight back to New York, he pressed again, "Let's definitely run when we get back to the city."

"Are you sure you want to run with me? I'll just slow you down," I worried aloud.

"I think it will be great to run with you. This is special," he insisted.

Thus began a beautiful friendship that lasted all the way to the West Coast where we would both find ourselves a decade later.

Triathlon Man

The Central Park Triathlon (CPT) is a short race, probably conceived for the weekend warrior—an enticement to future hardcore triathletes or a comfortable warm-up for experienced ones. The relatively short swim-bike-run dimensions of a quarter mile, twelve miles and five miles, respectively, require superb conditioning: competitors must remain in a continual sprint throughout the race. "No coasting allowed" became our mantra.

The most famous triathlon and one of the most grueling in the world is the Ironman Triathlon. A standard Ironman consists of a 2.4-mile swim, usually in ocean waters, followed by a 112-mile bike, finishing with a full (26.2 mile) marathon. Most athletes never contemplate running this race. Its proportions are nightmarish!

The CPT is much more benign in its dimensions than an "Ironman." As with many triathlons, it begins and ends in the same place. The staging area is located at the site of the giant Lasker recreational swimming pool in the northeast corner of Central Park. The staging area lies below ground level, permitting spectators to watch the beginning and end of the competition from the bleachers. Those who wish may leave the area to view the race from the cycling and running courses.

Race officials set up several bike racks against a fence at the south end of the pool. Before the race begins, they inspect all bicycles and properly tag them and their riders. Then racers place their bikes into the racks. I stationed my tandem against a fence alongside them as it didn't fit with the others.

The event director was open and gracious. Before applying, I spoke with her about my situation, expressing concern that either the officials or my fellow competitors might not think my using a tandem bicycle would be fair. "As long as you don't win the race," she quipped, "no one will mind your tandem." I assured her my swimming and running skills would more than offset any advantage I might have riding a bicycle built for two. Since I had apparently been green lighted by CPT officials, on race morning, my competitors expressed only curiosity about the tandem and sincere wishes of good luck, never questioning my right to be there.

In most such events, athletes arrive at the staging area at least an hour before race time. Numbers containing heat assignments are meted out based on information contestants provide about their swimming ability during the application process. (The honor system, plus reputation makes this a relatively fail-safe approach.)

The best athletes start in heat 1, and the worst in the final heat. Bar codes on the racing numbers contain correction factors that reconcile racers' finishing times with the starting time of their heat.

Experienced triathletes wear tight-fitting shorts and shirts that hold up as well when wet as when the wearer is on a bike or running. They place their shoes in toe clips on their pedals so they can leap upon their bikes, slip their feet into them, and take off without losing a second. I, on the other hand, had a dry shirt, socks, and running shoes waiting near my bike and lost as much as an entire minute in the transition.

My first triathlon, run in August 1989, drew attention from the public media. This attention benefited me through the rest of my running career.

My frequent cycling and running partner, Mary, thought the public should know that a blind person had entered the NY Central Park Triathlon. She called a friend who worked for the *NY Times*, and a few days later, a reporter met Mary and me at an upper West Side diner for an interview and photo shoot.

The interview went well. However, earlier that day, I had cut my forehead by bumping into a bent-over street sign. Embarrassed, I knew the photo accompanying the article would contain the visible blemish stamped in the top center of my mug.

The photographer took pictures of Mary and me riding the tandem, and Sharon joined us for the running shots. I forgot about the mark on my head. Instead, awareness was slowly surfacing. I was not eschewing publicity. Instead, I was happy to be engaging the media. Somehow, it was easy to accept that no matter how poorly I might place in the race, or even how self-conscious I might feel about the "stigmata" in the center of my forehead, I was having fun.

My plan for the triathlon was to swim without a guide, ride with Mary, and finish up running with Sharon. This meant I would have a fresh partner for each leg of the race.

The article hit the Saturday-morning *Times*. Ironically, because the race commenced at the crack of dawn, most readers didn't get to see the article until it had ended. However, about three miles into the run, an early bird spectator standing on the side of the course called out to me, "I saw your picture in the paper. Kick some butt, man!"

On race morning, with my stomach filled with butterflies, I met Mary at her Upper West Side apartment where we had stored the bicycle the day before. Together, we rode to the Lasker pool in the northeast corner of Central Park where Sharon awaited us. I cannot recall whether it was chilly that morning, but I do remember being unable to control my shaking.

The first heat lined up at the pool. Since, on my application, I had reported my quarter mile swim time conservatively, the race officials placed me in one of the last heats. With fifteen lanes roped off and three to five people per lane, more than one hundred racers had splashed their way out of the pool and mounted their bikes before I'd even started.

Since the lanes were three times longer than those in an Olympic pool, instead of nine relatively quick laps to the quarter mile, we swam three very long ones. I entered my lane with two others. I let them know I had poor eyesight and told them I would hug the side ropes to avoid head-on collisions. They said they would keep an eye out for me. The gun went off, and we swam forward.

Almost instantly, it felt as though I was alone in the water. In fact, after an initial flurry for position, I never saw my lane mates again.

I swam for what seemed like an eternity. Reaching a rope that traversed the end of the lane, I turned around, moved over to the right, and swam back. The rules prevented us from pushing off the wall, so when I reached the solid end of the pool, I couldn't use well-practiced spin turns. This slowed me down, but made little difference. (Later, I learned from Sharon that I was one of the slower swimmers in the pool.) I still had two more laps, but completed the quarter mile feeling quite refreshed, grateful I had trained at one half and three-fourths mile distances.

I scrambled out of the water. Mary stood with a towel and handed me my shirt, which I donned as she led me by the arm toward the bicycle. I had planned my transition poorly. Sitting on the ground to put on my running shoes cost me precious seconds.

Popping up, I grabbed the rear seat of the tandem, and we ran the bicycle to the edge of the staging area. Mounting near the exit, we sprinted toward the first hill.

I felt the bicycle accelerate on a short downgrade and shifted to the highest gear. Mary shouted, "There's a long hill in front of us." I waited until I felt the terrain level off and downshifted first to a middle and then to the lowest gear.

We rode steadily up and crested the north hill (the longest in Central Park). I wanted us to fly down the other side, but although a good rider, Mary disliked extreme speed. Her conservatism on downhills caused us to lose some time, but her willingness to work hard on uphills made up for most of it.

Central park is a great place for cyclists. Despite the antipathy that occasionally arises between runners and cyclists, I have always believed there is plenty of room for both—so long as the skateboarders and Rollerbladers don't clog up the works. The north, east, and west portions of the park are replete with steep and rolling hills sufficient to make all but ardent mountain bikers happy. At full tilt, the rolling hills seem much longer and steeper.

Two laps of the park later, we coasted into the staging area, dismounting and leaning the bike against our spot along the fence. The bike had performed flawlessly, gears shifting cleanly, tires remaining inflated, chain and derailleur well-behaved.

Sharon arrived immediately. Watching the race from the bleachers, she strolled to the spot where we parked the tandem, stretched in anticipation of the five-mile run she was about to undertake with me, and stood ready with tether in hand. I'll never forget my surprise and concern as we jogged onto the course. My legs felt as heavy as lead. Two circumnavigations of Central Park had left them wobbly. I panicked. "Would I be able to finish?"

Sharon suggested we jog slowly for the first half mile. This cleared us of the difficult north hill, leaving only rolling hills on the west side of the park and the famous "Cat" Hill running parallel to "Museum Mile" on the east side between Seventy-second Street and about Eighty-sixth Street and Fifth Avenue.

Named for a statue perched alongside the inner roadway, Cat Hill was often the final travail in most Central Park races. In the CPT, clearing the hill only signifies that another mile and a half lay ahead.

Running past the familiar start-finish line at Ninetieth Street, I began to feel exhilarated as I knew I'd topped the last major hurdle. All that remained was another mile with a peculiar left turn near 106th Street, placed there to add necessary distance to the course.

The path led us around a horseshoe turn and through a tunnel, ending at the top of a short flight of steps required to descend into the staging area. We chose to walk down the steps to avoid a last-minute crash. With the finish line only a hundred yards away, we were dismayed to see we had to make a tight right turn around the end of the swimming pool. This meant further loss of momentum as we slowed to make the turn. Tiptoeing around the corner, we ran toward the finish line. The cheers of spectators and scores of runners who had finished before me nearly brought tears to my eyes. It was over. I had done it. To my great satisfaction, I had even managed to finish in the middle of the pack. Only slightly more than half the participants finished the race in faster time.

Ready for My Close-Up

By the fall of 1990, I'd decided to sign up for the marathon again. This time, I told myself, I would run, not jog, the entire race. In October, I received a call from WABC television in New York.

They wanted to do a premarathon piece on me. The station had seen the triathlon article and thought a blind marathoner who also ran triathlons would make an interesting story for their premarathon coverage. Fully confident I would be running that year, I accepted the invitation.

I spent several hours with their reporter, Bill Evans, a runner who also doubled as a WABC meteorologist. Bill interviewed Robby and me. The camera crew took shots of us running and cycling. We rode the tandem up the north hill of Central Park while a camera crew rode perilously close to us in a van.

With Robby acting as guide, Bill jogged wearing a blindfold. Bill commented about the strange feeling of not being able to see his stride and foot placements. Had I known this conversation had taken place (Robby and Bill were out of earshot during their jog), I would have explained that, with only a little experience, blind people don't think about such things. The running motion is a natural part of human movement.

We commandeered a lane at the pool in the West Side YMCA. The producer wanted swim shots. Nearly getting into a fight with die-hard lunch-hour swimmers, we managed to keep a lane clear long enough for a camera woman, held tightly by her producer, to tip-toe along the edge of the pool, shooting down at me in the water as I swam lap after lap just beneath her. First, I bumped into the lane rope against which I always swam to avoid veering. "Swim straighter," she called. Then other swimmers, curious about what we were doing, insinuated themselves into the shots. The producer called out, "Swim another lap, please." Finally, the producer, noticing my fatigue and frustration, declared, "Okay, we've got it." All that effort translated into about ten seconds of actual footage.

Later in Harriet and Dennis's physical therapy office, the cameras rolled while they demonstrated techniques used to help heal my injuries and strengthen my vulnerable zones. Close-up shots show electrodes being placed on my leg at the site of "hot injury spots." Shots of Harriet massaging sore muscles and Dennis directing my use of various exercise machines rounded out the session.

The piece concluded on a poignant note. The viewer sees a head and shoulders shot of me talking about the one thing, as Bill Evans put it, "that still eludes him." While running in Brooklyn early in the marathon, I explain, "The children reach out to touch your hand or leg." Unfortunately, in my first marathon, even with my running partner's help, I kept missing their hand. I vowed, when I next ran that race, I would "touch the hand of a child."

As it turned out, I developed a sufficient number of minor injuries between the shooting and marathon day to give up the event that year. Although the station and television audience didn't know I wasn't among the approximately twenty-five thousand racers lining up at Fort Wadsworth, I felt guilty. I had accepted undeserved publicity. However, the fact that about 25 percent of the shots pertained to the complexity of being a blind person who happened also to be prone to running injuries enabled me to rationalize that I had contributed to public awareness. This was a good thing. Moreover, I had also contributed to the evolution of reality television. They simply hadn't seen the final episode yet!

In 1990, I ran the triathlon with Robby serving as both my biking and running partner, again, finishing somewhere in the middle of the pack. Mike and I would pair off to run the triathlons in 1991 and 1992.

A Hero Sandwich

Could I be dreamin'?
Is this really real?
'Cause there's something magic the way that I feel…

—(Alabama, "The Closer You Get,"
from *The Closer You Get*, 1983)

What do Tony Candela, Hank Aaron, Greg Laemond, Gary Carter, and Arthur Ashe have in common? Their names appear in the sports category on the 1990 National Hero Awards nomination ballot.

STAND UP OR SIT OUT

In 1989, Big Brothers/Big Sisters of America (BBBSA) joined forces with the Makers of Hero cologne to initiate the National Hero Awards. These awards honor people who have either inspired or been a boon to children and youth. The awards ceremony serves as a significant fund-raising event for BBBSA.

In 1990, spotting the *New York Times* article covering my participation in the Central Park Triathlon, the sponsors, needing a "civilian," added me to their list of sports heroes for 1990. With my name annotated as the first blind person to complete the NYCPT, I suddenly found myself placed alongside the names of some of the greatest sports stars of the modern era. I was convinced the gesture was purely honorary until I arrived at the awards banquet. They treated me like a king.

Sharon and I dressed in formal attire, and Hero Cologne sent a limo to carry us to the banquet. As soon as we entered the lobby of the Waldorf-Astoria, representatives from Hero Cologne and BBBSA greeted us and escorted us to the banquet room. Before we knew it, they introduced us to the leading nominee in the "music" category, Alabama. Pointing out the list of nominees, the representatives informed us the "leadership" category sported luminaries such as Julian Bond, George Bush, and Rudolph Giuliani. The "legendary" category showcased such greats as Jackie Robinson and Irving Berlin.

A few minutes later, a friendly and unassuming man approached us and said, "You must be the blind triathlete." The host of the event, Lynn Swan, Hall of Fame wide receiver from the Pittsburgh Steelers, spotting my cane, had zigzagged his way across the room to say hello.

Lynn was about my height, no extra fat that I could perceive, and still as solidly built as when he played football. The way he traversed the crowded room to greet me indicated he could probably still run pass patterns with the same agility as in his glory days with the Steelers. Lynn seemed to be in his element—charming, smooth, and warm in his approach to everyone with whom he spoke. He certainly made me feel like a "somebody."

Things got even better. No sooner had I asked if Hank Aaron were in the room than his massive hand gripped mine and a somewhat muffled hello wafted toward me. I couldn't tell if Hank was speaking softly or if I had passed into a fugue. I muttered something about hitting a baseball from a batting tee and how it wasn't nearly as much fun as swinging at a pitched ball. Hank chuckled, probably half in recognition and half out of politeness. 'I know what you mean."

Lynn suggested we pose for a photo. As we sat, shoulder to shoulder, leaning on our elbows upon a table, I could feel their muscles and the still-strong mass of their bodies reverberate through me. Although I felt dwarfed by their presence, the feeling was totally unlike those wrestling experiences where I had gotten trounced by my opponents. Enveloped in the moment, I was warmly aware of being unfrightened by their power.

No matter where I've lived since that dreamlike day, I happily parade visitors to the photo I proudly display on my wall. It shows a hero sandwich containing me with a smile on my face, bracketed by Lynn Swan on my right and Hank Aaron on my left. People tell me, although surrounded by two giants of the world of sport, I don't look as tiny as I felt.

We sat at beautifully adorned tables and were served a delicious meal. I don't recall what we ate. The first glass of champagne combined with the excitement sent me into a reverie. I thought about heroes I'd grown up with. Two stood out: the Yankees and, believe it or not, the crew of the starship *Enterprise*.

As a boy, I loved baseball. The Yankee dynasty was in full force when I became aware of the game. Those were the days of Mantle, Maris, Ford, Berra, and Howard. I grew into a devout fan, sneaking a small radio into bed at night to listen to Phil Rizzuto and Jerry Coleman broadcast the play-by-play. I would pray more for the Yankees to win than for the welfare of my soul. They brought peace to a sometimes troubled and often lonely boy.

There were many occasions in my childhood when I had no one to play with. I spent many fun-filled hours in mock ball games playing alone, hitting stones with a stick, and pretending to be the Yankees. On other occasions, I'd walk to a quiet place away from my immediate neighborhood—where no one could watch me—and played fantasy games of pitch and catch against a cinder block wall. The Yankees always won.

Through thick and thin, dry spells and championship runs, I've stuck with the Yankees. They've always been there, a constant source of joy and, during the eleven-year dry spell that began in 1965, a little frustration.

The same goes for the TV series *Star Trek*. An avid astronomy buff from the time I read my first book on the subject while convalescing from a broken arm at age twelve, *Star Trek* captured my fantasy with a power that continues to hold me to the present. Call it escapism, call it wonder about the potential of science to propel us to the stars, I have seen every television episode of the original series and all four spin-offs (five, if you count the cartoon series in the early '70s), not to mention every one of the movies. My attraction to this long-lived series mirrors that of so many "Trekors" and "Trekees." The *Star Trek* world portrays our society in a time when it has evolved to where excellence and power has thoroughly melded with benevolence and justice. Technology has mitigated the effects of severe disability. There is acceptance of all people without rancor and strain. The "prime directive" dictates noninterference with other cultures, and the crews of the various *Enterprise*s would sacrifice themselves rather than violate that rule.

The icing on the cake that evening was meeting Pam Dauber, of *Mork and Mindy* fame. As the event cohost, Pam impressed me as funny, quick, and gorgeous. A nice distraction occurred when the organizers surprised Ms. Dauber while she and Lynn conducted the ceremony. Unbeknownst to Pam, they had flown in her husband, Mark Harmon. As it happened, that day was her birthday, and Mark was the gift. A song by Alabama rounded out the evening.

One coincidence marred an otherwise perfect episode. The August 1991 issue of *People* magazine reviewed the event. Lists of the nominees in each National Hero awards category were presented along with a description of the fine work of BBBSA. I keep a copy of the issue among my treasured memorabilia. The fly in the ointment pertains to the magazine's cover photo of that issue: a shot of the infamous Jeffrey Dahmer. Unfortunately, Mr. Dahmer's grizzly escapades forever stand as a reminder that one man gone terribly astray can capture the front page in the popular media. If it weren't so tragic, the juxtaposition of Dahmer on the cover and us "do-gooders" in the center would be almost comical. I am pleased that *People* magazine didn't allow the Dahmer affair to detract from the work of the scores of people marching on much higher ground, who were honored on that mystical evening.

The Best for Last

In the August 1991 Central Park Triathlon, my bicycle chain came off twice during the race. Accompanied by lots of cursing, Mike and I managed to reposition it and keep racing. Although I finished the race, I did so with a poor showing. Toward the end of the run phase, Mike and I attempted to get down the steps leading to the pool area and finish line by running full tilt. Unrehearsed, we managed to stumble just enough to negate any time we would have saved over simply walking them.

Cursing our continued misfortune, Mike, as had been our wont when cross-country running, grabbed my arm and muscled me around the sharp right-hand pool turn. We sprinted hard across the finish line. Again, the crowd cheered us with exuberance. Disgusted, we left quickly and rode the bike directly to the repair shop.

In the 1992 triathlon, I ran slower than ever, having just come back from a second stress fracture to my right shin. However, stronger for having done a lot more swimming and bicycle training that summer, I popped out of the pool quicker; and Mike and I blew past many riders on the cycling course, making up time we would lose in the run. As we approached the menacing steps, Mike hooked his arm under mine. With a shout of "Now!," we hit the first step at full speed. A race official shouted, "No coaching," an admonition often reserved for superior athletes. Ignoring him, we cleared the steps in full stride.

Then we noticed a racer directly alongside, challenging us for position as we approached the final pool turn.

Mike has a competitive streak, which I appreciated at that moment. His favorite song is Billy Joel's "I Go to Extremes." Having run innumerable practices and several 10K, cross-country, and half-marathon races together, we only needed a split second to communicate that we would not permit our challenger to beat us to the finish line.

On other occasions, Mike's aggressive style caused us minor conflict on the race course. Once, about ten miles into the New Rochelle half-marathon, I grew so fatigued that I didn't want to run any more. Mike said, "Just run on your toes. That will rest your legs." Too tired to follow his suggestion, I told him we needed to slow down. "Keep running," he exhorted. Reasoning that were I running unattached, I would simply slow down, I decided to reclaim my race. Trusting in Mike's compassion, I dropped the tether and began walking, unattached and blind. "Are you crazy? What are you doing?" Mike growled, walking back to me. "Remember, this is my race," I shot back. He understood.

Mike's parents, native Irish, continually admonished their son to take good care of me while training on the streets of Riverdale. "Don't worry," he'd tell them, "I've got things under control."

Back at the triathlon, we kicked into high gear and streaked along the top of the pool. Again, because of our experience running under adverse conditions, we knew exactly how we would handle the ninety-degree right turn. Grabbing each other's hand, we cut the turn as close to the edge of the pool as we dared. This added a bit to the slight lead we had opened up on our competitor. Sprinting hard and hearing footsteps behind us, we focused on the finish line and screaming crowd ahead.

Everyone knew that the blind racer approaching the line was in a run for his life. So did I. The public address announcer told the crowd, "Here comes Tony Candela."

Our nemesis still tight on our heels, the image of the bulls of Pamplona filled my head, immediately replaced by the memory of the thundering hoard of "lead" runners catching and overwhelming me at the "Achilles Handicap" so many years ago. A sense of urgency surged through me. Mike perceived my determination. Driven by simultaneous rushes of adrenaline, Mike and I bent forward in unison, stretched our necks, and crossed the finish line at full stride. The sound of footsteps in pursuit had vanished.

That year, at age thirty-seven and in my final triathlon, I finished in 1.33:03, placing 69th out of 125 male finishers (at the 55th percentile). To put this in perspective, the last contestant to cross the finish line that year did so in 3:05:00. It turned out that the fellow behind me finished only one second later. Although much closer than I thought, it was of no consequence. It's on the record. I finally outran that bull!

Second Marathon

By November of 1991, I had maintained good running health long enough to sustain a concerted long-distance training regimen. Mike and I ran together regularly. At least once per week, we took the tandem for a ride across the Bronx to City Island and back—a quick twenty-miler, which we completed in an hour. I continued to run with Achilles and Safety Patrol and made it to the pool at Jack LaLanne's at least three times per week. On some days, I managed to get in a workout in two or even three of these activities. I was in great shape and ready for another try at a marathon.

I met a new running partner at the NYRRC. Jeff was an architect about my age who ran with grace and remarkable ease. One day, as we met for a run in the park, Jeff seemed euphoric. He happily reported that he had just run past the basketball player Isaiah Thomas. As Jeff ran past, Isaiah had complimented him on his form. "Nice stride, man."

Jeff was a confirmed bachelor whose apartment on the Upper West Side included an architect's table made of plywood, a futon, and two electrical guitars. Although soft-spoken by day, by night, Jeff played in a rock band that had managed to land a gig in a night club on the Lower East Side. The best thing about Jeff's apartment was its location just two blocks from an entrance to Central Park. He could practically fall out of his futon into an early morning workout.

STAND UP OR SIT OUT

It was around that time that Sharon and I started seeing signs that our relationship might be on the wane. For example, one day quite close to the marathon, she received a call from an old boyfriend. Unfortunately, I was visiting her at the moment and answered the phone. We never spoke about the incident, but somehow, the stresses and strains of our relationship had added up to a tacit understanding that we might soon be breaking up. Nevertheless, I was left with feelings of sadness and creeping anxiety about what it would be like to be "single" again. How could I engage the social world of running without Sharon? She had been my link to it since those halcyon days of postworkout pizza outings, we had danced together at more than a few Road Runners Club parties including a postmarathon gathering, and at least half my friends were hers.

On marathon morning, tensions were palpable. Neither of us spoke to each other as Robby, Sharon, and I rode the limo to Fort Wadsworth. As soon as we disembarked at the staging area, Sharon went off to join her friends.

I planned my marathon in two phases. Robby would run with me for the first half and Jeff the second. I learned a difficult lesson that day: never run a long distance race with a partner who isn't experienced reining you in if you exceed the pace agreed upon in premarathon planning.

Robby and I had done a twelve-miler ten days before the marathon and had run it a bit too fast. By marathon day, I was still feeling the effects of that run. This should have clued me to the need to reduce my pace, but once again, the excitement of the marathon blurred my perceptions.

The race commenced without a hitch. We ran through Brooklyn, me having explained to Robby that I absolutely had to slap hands with the children who might reach out to me. Unfortunately, when we got to the area where I thought they should be, Robby sympathetically reported that none of the children appeared to be venturing onto the course. I tucked my disappointment away; the echoing theme of *Rocky* being played by a band under an overpass just ahead helped me readjust my focus.

Meanwhile, my pace was still a few seconds per mile faster than it should have been. I didn't notice the fatigue slowly setting in. Perhaps the extra speed combined with sadness about missing the children and occasionally invasive thoughts about my waning relationship with Sharon had insidiously taken their toll because by time we'd reached the halfway mark and the rendezvous point with Jeff, I was exhausted.

"We can't stay here," Jeff exhorted as I told him how tired I was. "Let's get across the Fifty-ninth Street Bridge and then decide whether to finish the race." Robby indicated he would stick with us all the way if we wished and told me not to worry about dropping out if that is what I thought would be best.

We jogged to the Queensboro Bridge and walked the entire length across the East River. By time we reached First Avenue, I was sufficiently rested to tell Jeff and Robby it was my intention to finish the race.

I felt myself crying inside as we alternately walked and jogged toward the Bronx. Angry and frustrated at the exhaustion that threatened to defeat me, all I could think was that the problem from my wrestling days, a problem that for the most part I thought I had licked was dogging me again. I wanted to be mothered, to be held. Fortunately, Jeff didn't hear my moaning.

The monotony didn't abate. We walked the entire patch of the race that traverses the Bronx, gave forth with a good burst while circling Marcus Garvey Park, and settled back into a walk-run routine when we hit Fifth Avenue.

Meanwhile, Mike was having the best race of his life. Except for needing to run backward when he entered Central Park from Fifth Avenue, he reported having a wonderful time. His parents, sisters, and girlfriend were on First Avenue to cheer him on. There, he actually stepped off the course to give them a hug. Mike crossed the finish line in well under 3:20. I was about seventy minutes behind him.

As in my first marathon, as soon as we arrived at Central Park South, my spirits rose. I announced to Jeff and Robby, "I'm ready to run all the way in now." We accelerated, made our right and left turns, sprinted up the final hill to the deafening sound of the cheering crowd, and crossed the finish line. Ironically, my time was nearly the same as my first marathon two years earlier. However, the Mylar blanket felt just as warm, and the water and bagel, were it not for the nausea, would have tasted just as sweet.

Coming Home

If the quality of an experience or, for that matter, an entire effort were to be judged only by its outcome, my academic career receives a higher rating than my athletic one. After all, my academic record (I batted well above .900) far surpassed my wrestling and running accomplishments (around .500). Nonetheless, I value my athletic achievements more.

Over the years, the salve of time dulls the pain of injuries and losses, and selective memory accentuates the joy of teamwork and the thrill of victory. Thus I have placed my athletic career on a pedestal.

No matter how good or bad their record, scholar-athletes often struggle with conflicting feelings. If they admit that their love of athletics is as strong as academics, then they face the dilemma of how to balance the two. Those who understand the life of the scholar-athlete understand the constant juggling of time and energy such a life requires. Usually, giving more to one generally subtracts from the other. Most of us, I suspect, do not have sufficiently good time management skills to go full tilt in both arenas. Had I paid more attention to my wrestling career, I might have raised my won-loss record several percentage points. However, increased emphasis on sports probably would have diminished my scholastic output.

A senior year conversation with my assistant wrestling coach, Mr. McGuire, convinced me I had made the right choices. In response to my telling him I was worried about being late to practice because of National Honor Society commitments, he encouraged me to continue to take part in them. "You have to think about your future," he said. "Wrestling, at best," he reminded me, "will end when you graduate from college."

Visual impairment further complicated the demands on my energy. It made achieving academic excellence more difficult. Although throughout my high school years, I had enough vision to see the chalkboard and read textbooks and handwritten notes, I needed plenty of light, a front and center seat in the classroom, a magnifying glass, and about 25 percent more time to do my work.

As time went on, I drifted into using other adaptive techniques. For example, in my sophomore year, I discovered felt-tipped pens, a boon to anyone having difficulty reading notes taken in ballpoint pen. Felt-tipped pens produced thicker and darker lines. My eyes relaxed as soon as I began using them. Additionally, by my senior year, spurred on by the intense reading load of an Advanced Placement English class, I began using recorded books. In retrospect, it is clear to me that my vision was slowly and imperceptibly deteriorating and that I was expending a lot of energy to get by.

I did well on State Regents exams because I studied hard, and the exams were provided to me in large print. At that time, these exams determined final grades for most of the core courses I took and figured in the calculations for class standing. When the tallies came in, I had managed to place second in my class.

Then there were the dreaded SATs. The authorities allowed me to take these exams in a separate room from the rest of my classmates, with a proctor of my own and extra time. The proctor presented me with a large-print version of the test, a convention adopted for students just like me. There was some controversy for a while concerning special flagging of test results for students using these accommodations, but I don't think I was affected by them. The flagging was meant to demarcate the results as possibly having been obtained under circumstances that might confer either an advantage or disadvantage to those taking the test. (I've never learned which was on their mind, but I suspect the former.) Since even with large print I read slower than the average high school senior, I think giving me extra time was fair.

I scored high enough on the SATs, but not as high as I'd hoped. My scores got me into most of the colleges to which I applied, but not all of them. To my bewilderment, I learned that several of my classmates whose grade point average fell below mine scored a hundred points higher on the SATs than I did. This began several years of wondering whether I was as smart as I had always thought.

I may have been spooked by an event that occurred a year earlier. The PSATs (Preliminary Scholastic Aptitude Tests) did not arrive in large print. Inexperienced and foolishly undaunted, I attempted to take the test with the rest of my class and with no extra time. After an hour of struggling and my eyes tearing from strain and frustration, I decided to abandon ship. Packing up my papers, I stood, dropped the booklet on the proctor's desk, and without a word left the room. Strangely, neither I nor anyone else ever questioned how the system could have failed to catch me in its safety net at such a critical juncture. In fact, as I exited the examination room, no one even bothered to inquire why I was leaving.

In retrospect, I think this may have been a classic "Alphonse-Gaston" (a baseball fielding flub where each player looks at the other thinking he will catch the ball and they both let it drop to the ground). The guidance counselor might have thought my teacher of visually impaired students, itinerant and no longer a regular feature in my life, had handled the matter. For her part, she may have thought the guidance counselor had taken care of things. The upshot was that I never took the PSATs. This might have injured my academic career in that the PSATs were used both as a preparatory exam for the all-important SATs and as a screening tool for the prestigious National Merit Scholarships. Fortunately, I had other funding for college, a boon in that the odds of winning a National Merit Scholarship were quite slim anyway.

Although visual impairment only slightly attenuated my academic achievement, it is hard to estimate just how much it mitigated my skill as a wrestler. Poor eyesight, for example, lessened my self-confidence and, perhaps, the confidence others had in me. This, in turn, might explain why it never dawned on me or my coaches that I should attend summer wrestling clinics as did many high school wrestlers. Also, the fact that I didn't use the "touch-start" technique until I got to college meant I never learned to overcome the disadvantage of seeing my opponent poorly during the takedown part of my matches. Had I embraced this rule and developed special takedown techniques, I might have molded an advantage out of a disadvantage.

Visual impairment definitely affected my social life. Although it is difficult to separate one's personality from the influence of adults and the attitudes of children and the interaction of all three, in elementary and junior high school, I had rocky social relations with many of my peers. My lashing out at those who tormented me only served to exacerbate their teasing, taunting, and name-calling. I retain memories of "stolen" lunch bags and books, being picked last for gym class and neighborhood ball games, and continuous worry that my untrustworthy vision might fail me at inopportune moments. Tripping up or down stairs or failing to recognize a face, to name only two of many mishaps that befall people with partial vision, caused embarrassment for me and more teasing from the kids.

Thankfully, by mid–high school, due in part to their growing maturity and mine, I began to build normal social relationships with my peers. As a member of the wrestling team, I not only made friends with my teammates but also with several respected members of the football, basketball, track, and baseball teams. Some of my acquaintances were three-letter athletes, and a few of them decided to be my "guardian angels." For example, my social status rose immensely whenever a star athlete said hello to me in the hallway or occasionally came to my rescue when an unaware bully gave me a hard time. School, which once signaled discomfort, became a much more pleasant place to be.

The one area where I was handicapped was girls. I didn't drive and was uncertain about whether I could function in many social situations like dances, dining out, and the movies. I was also a bit shy. On the other hand, I was undaunted asking and getting dates to both my junior and senior proms. Dad drove us to the venues.

My High School

North Rockland High School (NRHS) opened for business in September of 1969. I commenced my junior year in the splendor of a shiny new facility that contained, among other niceties, an

Olympic-style swimming pool, a planetarium, modern weight-lifting machines, and a state-of-the-art wrestling room. Lectures for chemistry class were held in the planetarium. The physics teacher took advantage of the fact the planetarium could be completely darkened to demonstrate newly acquired laser technology. While he sprinkled chalk dust all over the place, we watched, fascinated as the lasers illuminated the dust as it scattered on the podium, the floor, and all over our teacher. This inspired us to incorrigibility. One day, much to his chagrin, by the time the dust settled, the laser faded, and the planetarium lights came back on line, we had sneaked out of the room. There he stood, alone and looking like a ghostly apparition.

The wrestling room came complete with wall-to-wall padding and an independently controlled thermostat that enabled us to practice in ninety-degree temperatures—a tradition borne out of the need for heat to guard against muscle injuries and our desire to sweat off pounds to qualify for lower weight classes. Most of us wanted to weigh as little as possible so we wouldn't be at a strength disadvantage in comparison to our opponents who we knew also cut weight just as vigorously.

Packaged into the new school were long traditions carried from its predecessor, Haverstraw-Stony Point High School. For example, the trophy case near the main office contained memorabilia of great athletes of yore, including my Uncle John, who in the early 1960s was a champion wrestler. His coach sired a son, Chuck, who as a member of my cohort became an excellent wrestler for NRHS.

Chuck and I practiced together a great deal and occasionally competed for the same varsity spot. He won all such matches. As a senior, I tutored his younger sister in algebra. My tutoring helped her do well on the Regents' exam. I graduated in 1971; Chuck graduated two years later. I didn't see him again for twenty years, running into him in a most unusual place.

Helen Hayes

Robby and I continued to run and swim together. In the spring of 1990, he came up with another great idea. "Why don't you run the Helen Hayes Classic?" he asked. He explained that Helen Hayes Hospital, a rehabilitation facility in my hometown, West Haverstraw, and named after the great actress who donated a great deal of money to it, held an annual 10K race as a fund-raiser. Actually, I knew a great deal about this hospital. Decades before, my father, rehabilitating after one of his numerous back surgeries, earned his high school equivalency diploma there. I obtained my first formally paid job there—a summer position as a floor mopper and window washer. I even took a college child psychology course there in the summer of 1974. Most important, her nest empty, my mother, returning to the workforce, ably served in its housekeeping department for more than seventeen years. Today, the hospital is affiliated with the NY-Presbyterian hospital system.

The race was unique in that it catered to runners with disabilities, especially Achilles runners. Three major categories ("disabled ambulatory," "disabled nonambulatory," and "nondisabled") were established for the race. Members from each category commenced the race at different times in an attempt to increase competition among the categories to reach the finish line first. Robby and I traveled to West Haverstraw and entered the 1990 Helen Hayes Classic. I had a bad run but learned a lot about the course. Vowing to avenge my poor performance, I signed up for the 1991 race.

Shortly before the race, I received a call from Jamie Kempton, a reporter with the *Rockland Journal News*. Informing me he was an avid runner himself, Mr. Kempton asked if he could do a story about me. He said that his readers would be interested in a blind Rockland County native coming home to run in the Helen Hayes race. Having learned to appreciate the benefits of publicity, I agreed to do the story. The article came out the day before the race.

Following my lead and containing a comment from my Achilles coach, Dick Traum, the article predicted I would finish second in the "disabled ambulatory" category. I knew of one runner who could beat me—if he were in shape. Since I had heard rumors that he wasn't, I secretly thought I had a chance to win. I entered the race in excellent shape, having run the Brooklyn half marathon only a month earlier.

Robby and his wife, Aileen, drove me to Stony Point, where my parents had moved a few years earlier. My father, reading the *Journal News* prediction, thought I had overestimated my chances. I told him that if my archrival was not in shape, I thought I could do even better. He shook his head and smiled.

We trooped to the staging area behind the hospital and, contrary to race protocols, I insisted on starting with the nondisabled runners. This was what I'd always done and, since the Achilles Handicap in 1989, I had no desire to relive the "running with the bulls" experience by starting early and having the real lead pack overtake me. Robby agreed, suggesting to me that we might have to politic with race officials afterward to collect my first place award should it come to that.

The weather was perfect, and the race started with the usual jostling and maneuvering of hundreds of runners packed like sardines at the starting line. Robby and I were an experienced team and started at a smooth, even pace. We picked our spots, judiciously deciding when to pass runners by zigzagging around them. Early in a race, you don't want to do any more than necessary to get a clear lane in which to run at your desired pace. Too many maneuvers add distance and unnecessarily drain your energy.

Clearing the hospital grounds and taking to the familiar roads of Thiells, a hamlet adjacent to West Haverstraw, Robby and I rehearsed the course. I reminisced about running a lesser approximation of the course as part of cross-training for high school wrestling. "In those days, I never thought I could run the kind of distance we're running today," I explained to Robby. "Until I got to college," I elaborated, "I hadn't run more than a mile or two at a time."

The square course took us right past NRHS and, a few miles later, back to the hospital staging area. Approximately a mile into the race, we passed my arch Achilles rival, who, Robby informed me about twenty minutes later, looked tired. I asked him why he hadn't told me at the time and he said he didn't want me to get too excited and drain myself prematurely. "Didn't we agree on our pace?"

About then, I heard someone call my name. Turning my face to "look" over my right shoulder, the voice, already fading behind us, called out, "It's Mr. Singer." It was my senior class math teacher. He was now Doctor Singer, having earned a law degree in the interim. Twenty years earlier, Mr. Singer introduced me to calculus, analytical algebra, and probability theory. Little did I know that a decade later, these disciplines would help me get through graduate-level statistics. Spotting me almost too late, he had apparently recognized my receding profile in time to call my name.

A mile from the finish line, I ran into Chuck, my high school wrestling friend and rival. He was part of a slightly faster pack that had slowly overtaken me. Cruising up on my left side and touching my arm, he said, "Hello, Anthony." (That's what half the people called me until I got to college.) "It's Chuck." Surprised, yet instantly recognizing his voice, I reached out, grabbed his still-muscular arm, and asked him how he was doing. Chuck said he was doing great and that it was good to see me. Suggesting we talk at the finish line, he slowly moved ahead. I didn't see him afterward, but the paper reported Chuck finished about thirty seconds before me. That made his pace about five seconds per mile faster than mine. Chuck was an even better wrestler.

We passed the five-mile marker, and Robby said he hadn't seen another "disabled ambulatory" runner in quite some time. It was possible, he announced, that I was the category leader. This buoyed me. I noticed my stride lengthen, my breathing smoothen, and my overall posture become more upright than it had been for a mile or so.

We turned left on the final approach to the hospital grounds and the finish area. Knowing my training would hold me in good stead, I told Robby it was time to pump it up. We increased our speed until my breathing became labored. My race was exactly where I wanted it to be.

Maintaining an accelerated pace, we passed dozens of runners, an excellent indicator of a great run. Leaving the straightaway we'd been on for several hundred yards, we made first a right turn and then a final hard left. The finish line lay directly ahead. We kicked into an all-out sprint, passing through the finish zone at full speed. I had indeed won my category in the Helen Hayes Classic.

The race officials were gracious and didn't scold me for starting with the main pack. The award consisted of an inscribed bowl and a $300 prize. I also was happy because, for the second and only other time in my life, my mother had seen me emerge triumphant from a rough competition. Eighteen months later, having completed my last race, the 1992 NY Central Park triathlon, and "retiring" from racing, I used the winnings to buy a treadmill.

National Honor Society

In my junior year (1970), my academic accomplishments bore fruit. I was inducted into the National Honor Society along with many of the kids with whom I'd attended class since junior high. Eligibility for the society required at least a 90 percent academic average and good citizenship. The induction ceremony requires Honor Society seniors, bearing candles, to go into the audience to tap new members on the shoulder. They escort them to the stage where the new members take seats of honor. Speeches are made about leadership, trust, and other desirable traits; and a keynote speaker regales the assembled masses (including proud parents, siblings, and the entire student body and faculty) with reminiscences and pearls of wisdom.

I was elected Honor Society president in my senior year. My short-lived legacy was a soda machine placed in the cafeteria. Two years later, succumbing to resistance from cafeteria staff that had started immediately after I announced we had gotten permission from the principal to install it, the principal order the machine removed. "These kids should be drinking milk," the nutritionist scolded. All I could see were potential club revenues and popularity for Honor Society members who were regarded as elitists by many in the student body. So much for my wisdom!

A more appropriate legacy was the creation of a policy where society members were granted unlimited pass privileges so they could move about the school building unmolested by hall monitors. The qualities of leadership, trust, and other desirable traits that made us worthy of being Honor Society members, I argued, made us worthy of the privilege of free movement within the school. The administration agreed.

In six months of actual operation, we made enough money from the soda machine to donate $1,000 to the library, a tidy sum for 1971 and $300 in scholarships. We also managed to leave a solid treasury for the upcoming class. So much for their wisdom!

Early in the fall of 1991, while planning the next induction ceremony, the Honor Society faculty advisor, Mrs. Pedri, commenced her search for a keynote speaker. Leafing through lists of alumni, she saw my name and recalled seeing both the article in the *Rockland Journal News* about my running in the Helen Hayes 10K Classic and the television piece that preceded the 1990 NYC Marathon. She wondered if the blind fellow who was the subject of these pieces might be the same person listed as graduating from NRHS in 1971. Lurking deeper in her memory was the image of a very little boy—one she thought she knew a very long time ago. Wondering if these three pieces of information were connected to the same individual, Mrs. P. called me.

When I told her I was indeed the Anthony Candela who once attended NRHS, she astounded me by telling me she knew me when we both lived in Haverstraw in 1954, the year my poor eyesight became evident. She was a six-year-old girl at the time and recalled that my aunt and uncle knew her parents. In the intervening years, Mrs. Pedri completed her education, married a fellow teacher, and fashioned a successful career in the community in which she had grown up.

Mrs. P. asked me to give the keynote speech at the 1991 National Honor Society induction ceremony. Flattered and happy to have a chance to give back to my old high school, I accepted her invitation.

The kids were great. I'd been away so long that I was surprised to see so many people with whom I'd grown up—including several of my old teachers. When you live in New York City, you tend to forget that most of the people in the world live their lives close to the place in which they spend their childhood. One young woman inductee was the daughter of a childhood friend. I saw three of my four history teachers, including Mr. McGuire, my junior varsity wrestling coach.

My eleventh grade Spanish teacher slapped me on the shoulder, still recalling the time I successfully and extemporaneously taught a class for him during senior class teaching day.

One person from my past said hello to me, not by words, but through a grand gesture. Mrs. Pedri introduced me as keynote speaker, recalling the detective work required to find me and reminding the audience that this man who worked full-time, studied for his doctorate, and ran marathons had sprung from seeds sown at NRHS. As I approached the podium, unbeknownst to me, someone in the rear of the auditorium rose to his feet. Although I was vaguely aware that the applause seemed to last a long time, unable to see the audience, I didn't know that the man in the back of the room had gestured for everyone to rise to their feet. It was the now-head football Coach Casarella, the man who had protested my loss in a pivotal high school wrestling match twenty years earlier, still rooting for me.

In my keynote, I reminisced and spouted pearls of wisdom, recalling the days we sat and argued about the justness of the war in Vietnam, whether Lieutenant Calley was really guilty of murder, and worries about the draft. I spoke about the technologies that high school kids took for granted in 1991 that didn't even exist in 1971. I concluded by explaining that while times and technology may change, the single constant in history is humanitarian love. Without love, I declared, everything else holds little meaning. I encouraged the inductees and everyone in the audience to take care of each other, explaining that I wouldn't have gotten as far as I did without people having taken care of me.

That day, the glow in my soul was rekindled. Without realizing it, I had given both the audience and myself a message. If we let them, negative emotions from the past can fade with time. We must make the most of our memories. They should build us up, not tear us down. If we can find the good in everything that happens to us, even losing an important wrestling match, we will continue to strive and flourish.

Ages of a Man

> When I was a child I spoke as a child
> I understood as a child I thought as
> a child; but when I became a man
> I put away childish things.
>
> —1 Corinthians 13:11

In April, 1992, about a month after running the Brooklyn Half, a now-familiar throb in my right shin appeared to be worsening. This time, it took only a few practice runs for the pain to override denial and convince me that I would again be sidelined. A stress fracture of my right tibia, only millimeters from the one I sustained in 1989, took me off the road and back to the physical therapy office.

Decision

> That's me in the corner
> That's me in the spotlight
> Losing my religion
> Trying to keep up with you
> And I don't know if I can do it… (REM, "Losing My Religion" from *Out of Time*, 1991)

A 10K race on Roosevelt Island provided the coup de grâce. Sharon and I signed up for what sounded like a fun time running on fast and flat territory on a long, narrow strip of land nestled in the waters of the East River between Manhattan and Queens. We took the tram at Fifty-ninth and Second Avenue, a thrilling ride because of the tram's mild oscillation as it crosses high over the eastern edge of Manhattan and the water of the East River. On one side, you can watch the cars crossing the Queensboro 59th Street Bridge; on the other, you can look past the projection of Roosevelt Island all the way to the bifurcating sections of the Robert F. Kennedy Triborough Bridge some four miles to the north.

We touched down on Roosevelt Island. Formerly Welfare Island, this 147-acre landmass stretches from north to south and is under the jurisdiction of the borough of Manhattan. It once held prisons but now is home to hospitals, sports facilities, and a variety of housing developments. Runners often seek "personal bests" there as its flatness inspires speed. Most of us, failing to pace ourselves properly, end up exhausted at the end, disappointed in our race times, and dragging our butts across the finish line, breathing harder than we had intended. This happened to Jeff and me in a 10k race we ran in the Ironbound section of Newark a year or so before. After the race, we drowned our sorrows in sangria and Portuguese paella.

Sharon and I knew my chances of actually starting the 10K that day were less than stellar. I had experienced sharp, pulsing pain in a well-defined place on the front of my right shin for a few weeks and hadn't been able to run more than a mile for a week. I knew from previous experience that my dread of downhill terrain and yearning for pain-free uphill running was a definite indication of a stress fracture.

We tried a few practice jogs near the staging area of the race. The pain asserted itself, and I reluctantly agreed to wait on the sidelines while Sharon joined the race. The hour or so I sat alone was a pivotal point in my running career.

I listened to music blaring from the public address system and contemplated my future. As the throngs of racers passed me and disappeared into the distance, my addiction to running disappeared with them. By the time Sharon rejoined me, having run a good race, I had arrived at two separate, but related, conclusions.

Sharon and I had begun to see the parting of the ways several months earlier. I had grown frustrated, unable to fully accept that she didn't want as much from our relationship as I did. Once in a restaurant in the World Financial Center, I actually asked her to marry me. She declined. We broke up for a few months after the 1991 Marathon and then reunited. During our breakup, I realized I had gotten too emotionally dependent upon her. In fact, while we were separated, it hurt so much that I obtained a referral to a psychiatrist. He prescribed a short regimen of Prozac. I took the antidepressant for a few months, discontinuing it when Sharon and I temporarily reunited. I disliked the side effects and vowed I would never take such medication again.

It took some time, but I finally understood that my attachment to Sharon had grown unhealthy. While I sat alone, waiting for her to return from the race, a popular song from the group REM twice repeated itself over the bullhorn. I took this as a sign. Although I worried my decision to break up with Sharon was unilateral, when we discussed it, Sharon told me she felt the same way and thought it would be for the best if we no longer dated. Of course, as soon as she said this, I immediately began to feel lonely.

That day, I also decided that it was time for me to rethink my running career. I'd originally taken up running with two goals in mind: fitness and improved mental health. Although more fit than I had been since college wrestling (and lighter in weight), my mental outlook, at least toward running, had become tainted by the pain of injuries and disappointment at not being able to achieve to my talent level. All that did was bring back my lifelong struggle with self-disappointment. I was convinced that had my right leg stayed as healthy and strong as my left, I could have run faster, finishing races at least tenth percentile points higher in the ranks.

The inextricable link between running and my relationship to Sharon didn't help matters. Sharon and I had trained together, ate, slept, and talked running for two solid years. Most of my friends were somehow identified with the world of running. Without Sharon, I felt neither running nor my social life would ever be the same. As impossibly difficult as I thought it would be, I had to let both of them go.

Breaking up with Sharon proved as difficult as I thought it would. Over the two years we dated, Sharon and I spent countless hours together running, attending awards ceremonies and dances hosted by running clubs and friends, traveling together, and sharing a roller-coaster ride of romantic feelings interspersed with ambivalence. We were hot and cold. Much as a mouse in a maze receiving intermittent reinforcement from B. F. Skinner, I had become attached to Sharon in ways that made it seem like I could never emotionally survive without her.

Although my relationship with Pat had disintegrated nine years earlier and my breakup with Joan five, I had not fully exorcised memories of the pain I felt after each breakup. I believed I didn't have the strength to go through that pain again. How, I asked myself, could I exist without Sharon? I decided to follow the old, if not ill-advised, adage: "The best way to forget one woman is to find another." Luckily, a path appeared before me.

A New Road

A month before making the "decision" to break up with Sharon, I met Jamie, a cute cherry-blonde woman and nonrunner, who had recently joined my staff at the Commission for the Blind. Jamie exuded a vivacious approach to life. Although I found myself attracted to her, our working relationship and my attachment to Sharon prevented me from allowing those feelings to deepen. I hung out with her at work, perhaps giving her a little more than her fair share of my supervisory attention. A month after the stress fracture sidelined me and I had broken up with Sharon, I asked Jamie for a date.

In my idleness, I continued swimming, spending lots of time with Jamie and as much time cycling with Mike as I could. With my enthusiasm for the rigors of everyday training diminished, I decided to use the summer of 1992 to prepare for two last races. I selected the Bronx Half Marathon in July and the Central Park Triathlon in August.

During my "convalescence" and retraining, Jamie and I fell in love. We ate lunch together; she treated me to a Neil Diamond concert, and we vacationed in Lake George. I received a promotion at my job, and we hired a supervisor to replace me. Thus I no longer directly supervised Jamie. My supervisor agreed to handle any personnel-related issues.

Meanwhile, with money from a divorce settlement, she made a down payment on a house in a lovely village on Long Island's North Shore. Having made appropriate arrangements at work to avoid conflict of interest, we agreed to move into the house together the following September.

I had methodically assembled the pieces that would comprise the next phase of my life. My ambivalence toward the running life probably clouded my perception. I failed to realize that the round-trip commute from Long Island to the city would absorb four hours per day. Leaving for work at the break of dawn and getting home after seven o'clock effectively ended my running career. Moreover, I developed a single-minded obsession with house management and family building. These combined to turn my attention from the running trails to home and hearth.

Last Hurrahs

My final road race was quite enjoyable. The Bronx Half Marathon, a race I ran three times in my career, seemed to always take place on a hot day. Unlike previous half marathons, I had no allusions of scoring a personal best in this race. My second stress fracture had healed, but I hadn't returned to the form that once enabled me to run half marathons at better than a 7:40 pace. "No," I told Mike, with whom I'd run most of my half marathons. "I won't be doing this half in under 1:42. This will have to be a fun run."

Two things made this particular race special. First, it began and ended around Yankee Stadium. Second, both Mike and I each had a fan along the race course.

The old Yankee Stadium was a wonder to behold. A classic twentieth-century-styled baseball stadium, the house that Ruth built stood as a monument to the roots of baseball. I recall as a child driving past the stadium on the Major Deegan Expressway en route to either the eye doctor in Manhattan or relatives in Queens. Inside, the image of pattern-cut green grass, orange-colored infield dirt, pure-white bases and lines, and, in the 1960s, the Ballantine Beer sign remain forever etched in visual memory. I can easily retrieve the sounds of bat on ball, ball hitting glove, Bob Sheppard's public address announcements, and the overwhelming din of hometown fans—in my opinion, the best, most loyal, and smartest baseball fans in the world.

My personal fan club during the Bronx Half consisted of one of my secretaries who lived in an apartment overlooking the Grand Concourse, the wide boulevard comprising a large chunk of the course. The race traveled north on the Concourse, wound its way around a reservoir, back south on the Concourse, ending in a sprint to the finish area. Hearing her call my name from a perch in a tall apartment building—both coming and going—buoyed me on a hot day when, not in great running shape, I had to struggle to complete the 13.1 mile trek. Except for some walking on part of the return route, the race went better than expected.

Somewhere near the reservoir, Mike's fan club—his father—stood waiting to see his son escorting the blind fellow whom he had never met in person. All he had to go on was the sound of my voice when I called for Mike by telephone and the stories Mike told of our running adventures. As for me, I loved his Irish accent and could easily discern where Mike got his warmth and kindness.

Proud of Mike for his accomplishments as a compliance officer with several large corporations, Mike's father was even more proud of him for his generosity. In his mind, Mike's running with me was an example of good old Irish charity. To his credit, Mike would straighten out anyone (except his father) who thought he ran with me as an act of charity. "I really enjoy running with you," he always said.

In retrospect, the half marathon distance (13.1 miles) turned out to be optimal for me. Given the amount of training I could do and the limits on weekly mileage placed upon me by my tender tibia and knee, the distance was one I could run all the way at full stride. With experience, I figured out that my natural wall resided at around fifteen miles. My tendency toward injury and difficulty in finding running partners truncated my training just enough to prevent me from adequately preparing for races beyond the wall. Thus at 13.1 miles, the half marathon was ideal and will forever have a warm place in my heart.

Mike and I finished the Bronx Half only a few minutes slower than my average. Sitting in the grass of a nearby park awaiting the awards ceremony, our lack of chatter and banter spoke volumes. We knew, except for the triathlon the following month, this was most likely going to be our last race together. We agreed to run and ride as much as possible during the intervening weeks, and a month later, we ran the 1992 Central Park Triathlon. Then I hung up my gloves.

"Supercrip"

In 2001, a well-known blind person, Erik Weihenmayer, successfully climbed to the top of Mount Everest. He has since climbed the highest peaks on all seven continents, accomplished several tandem cycling feats, and white-water kayaked the Grand Canyon. His exploits made all the major newspapers, and Erik, a former elementary schoolteacher, became an icon and, yes, a motivational speaker.

Erik's success spurs debate among blind people. What they argue about is the image of the "supercrip," a term that describes high-achieving people with disabilities. These individuals not only make it onto the public radar, they create an aura that anything is possible if—despite incredible odds—you try hard enough. Unfortunately, their accomplishments plant in the minds of many that anyone with a disability who is not a high-achiever is somehow deficient.

Some blind people argue that Erik's image paints an unachievable picture for the rest of us who, as with the general public, will not achieve the summit, no matter how hard we try. Although wonderful individuals, "supercrips," while making us proud and inspiring us, inadvertently set up expectations most of us cannot achieve. To his credit, along with Paul Gordon Stoltz, his co-author in their book "The Adversity Advantage," Erik recognizes that we are not all built the same. Some of us are "campers" achieving and then seeking equilibrium, while others are "quitters" and the most adventurous of us are "climbers".

The achievements of "climbers" kick up guilt in me. I have often wondered what deep-seeded faults keep me from achieving what they have achieved. "You've got to want it bad enough," so goes the familiar refrain. I am glad Stoltz and Weihenmayer differentiate between "everyday greatness", that which most of us do when we turn adversity to advantage versus "epic greatness", like that of Erik and his mountain-climbing and kayaking teams.

In the end, supercrips expand our knowledge and even expectations of what is ultimately possible. Non-believers begin to believe and sometimes give people with disabilities a chance when they may not have done so. For the average person however, the most valued role models are those with whom regular folks can identify. I hope as an all-around regular guy, I will be one of those models.

Stoltz and Weihenmayer describe taking what might be for some an impediment and using this 'adversity advantage' to energize and propel our actions forward. They suggest purposely placing ourselves into adversity as a strengthening tool. This I have done on numerous occasions. I credit my father for teaching me to feel uneasy about quitting, my mother for the inner drive to seek equilibrium, and both of them for sowing the seed inside me that has enabled me to be an occasional climber.

In 1992, I decided that I couldn't be a supercrip anymore. Oddly enough, the term comes from a genuine attempt to countervail the detrimental effect of the word *cripple*, which over the years has given us the image of a person totally incapable of performing even the most basic physical or mental tasks. The term is used by a newly developing specialty, disability studies. The field began back in the early 1980s, coincidentally, about the time I commenced my own supercrip career. It was then, while working full-time, I started my doctoral program. Commencing a ten-year process of driving myself to the point of exhaustion, not willing to accept that I might have limitations, I pushed the envelope as far as I could.

Despite my divorce from Pat having altered the game plan, I pushed on. Things grew difficult without her support. Lonely and scared, I learned to fend for myself. Despite the difficulties, I managed to learn to downhill ski, complete my doctoral courses and qualifying exams, get through a vigorous clinical internship, and begin a dissertation. Adding long-distance running and moving from relationship to relationship really stretched the envelope. By the time I met Jamie, I was ready for a change of pace.

Among the loose ends was property I had purchased in Riverdale. In 1988, I took out a thirty-year mortgage and purchased a co-op apartment. In September of 1992, after living there only four years, I sublet the apartment and moved into a house with Jamie.

The house (and a second mortgage) was near the Port Jefferson line of the Long Island railroad. The lengthy commute combined with lifestyle changes that go with married life made me a couch potato.

Choosing not to establish running connections on the Island, I reduced my running to meeting Adria and Kay in Central Park once a week for safety patrol. This routine lasted about a year. I set up the tandem on a training stand in the garage and made it into a stationary bicycle. A treadmill sat alongside the tandem. They got only occasional use.

Jamie was only recently divorced from a lonely marriage. Fearing abandonment yet again, she asked me to stay close to home. "After I'm comfortable that you won't spend too much time away from me," she asserted, "I'll feel better about your going back to running." I began to enjoy the more relaxing and pain-free suburban lifestyle.

House of Cards?

Life marches on. Things change. After a while, Kay moved to Philadelphia, and Adria and I decided to end our volunteer work with the safety patrol. A few years later, I lost touch with Robby, Mary, and Jeff. Two years later, in 1997, Mike moved to San Francisco to take a job with a lucrative investment firm and to be closer to his girlfriend, Diane, whom he met in Los Angeles on a business trip a few years earlier.

I gained lots of weight and grew ambivalent about my new lifestyle. Having to change over my wardrobe twice in a three-year period made me angry. Although it felt good being pain-free, I mourned the loss of my physique. Joining Weight Watchers in 1995, I dropped twenty of the forty pounds gained since April of 1992. Increasing my treadmill and stationary bicycling activity helped a little, but it was clear I had truly retired from concentrated athletics.

In 1993, I made another difficult decision. My career going well and my dissertation progressing slowly, I decided to end my program at NYU. Although continuing to work on it, my doctoral dissertation had taken a back seat. A decade had elapsed since I began the program, and the university now required me to explain why I hadn't finished within the required ten-year time frame. I completed an application for a one-year extension, writing that I was making good progress on my dissertation proposal and citing changes in the makeup of my dissertation committee as the source of my delays.

Indeed, over the past four years, my first committee chair took early retirement due to illness, and one member left the university to do private consulting. My "theory man," another member of my committee, was transitioning his career and growing bored with the cognitive-behavioral approach that undergirded my dissertation project. NYU, committed to its doctoral students completing their programs, accepted my application for extension and offered support in the form of dissertation groups and coaching from faculty.

Another year passed. In 1993, soon after returning from my honeymoon with Jamie, a large bill and another request for extension came due. I decided my life was sufficiently satisfying to pack it in. In retrospect, as much as I wanted the doctorate and the opportunity to study psychology in depth, part of my motivation for entering the program may have been to compete with Pat and to satisfy my father.

My committee chair tried to talk me out of resigning, but I'd lost interest and felt that, with two mortgages to pay, I couldn't afford the earnings loss that acceptance of a position as a "freshman" psychologist would bring. (In fact, had I become a psychologist, I would have lost as much as $20,000 per year of first year income in 1993 dollars.) Although this decision still makes me sad (I loved everything about both the study and practice of psychology and believed I had a natural talent for the field), it wasn't all for naught. The skills I learned while in the program have helped me in my career. I have received promotions and salary increases, I have published and assisted in research projects, and I have made a name for myself in my field.

When I told him the news, my father bore his disappointment silently. He'd been going through a bad time himself, his physical problems exacerbated by psychological difficulties I attribute to long years of back pain and, believe it or not, his cessation from smoking. A thyroid cancer scare caused him to stop, but in my opinion, failure to realize that cigarette smoking had provided him a medicinal benefit led to the development of a full-fledged anxiety disorder. It felt unnatural, when I told him, that he didn't protest my leaving the doctoral program.

In 1995, I initiated another monumental life change. Promoted to a management position and transferring to a new office, I decided that I had risen as far as I was going to within the New York State bureaucracy. I took advantage of a downsizing movement, left state service, and went to work for Lighthouse International (now Lighthouse-Guild), a large and powerful agency for the blind in the New York City-Metropolitan area.

While other not-for-profit agencies were cutting back, the Lighthouse portfolio enabled it to move forward. I became a mid-level manager, directing its employment-related services. There, I worked my fingers to the bone.

In 1999, with financial problems mounting, Jamie and I broke up. My growing ambivalence about suburban living and loss of physique and fitness as I moved through my midforties made me grouchy. Jamie's longing for something or someone to fulfill an empty place inside her made her a less attentive spouse. We spent money on vacations, home improvements, the car, and lots of champagne (our favorite of spirits). Debt accrued as we renovated first this and then that part of the house. Finally, credit card bills and loan payments reached a breaking point—and so did we.

It wasn't all negative. In the seven years we were together, we took more than a dozen major vacations. Although debt-producing, the trips were nonetheless quite enjoyable. We cruised to Alaska, the Panama Canal, western Mexico, and Scandinavia. Trips to Paris and Egypt have forever enriched my life. Our final cruise to Bermuda was a bust; we fought and had a terrible time. Our marriage was teetering on the edge when shortly after our return from the ill-fated cruise, an old boyfriend of Jamie's suddenly reappeared. This set us firmly on the road to divorce.

During the breakup period, I sought solace once again in medication. This time, I convinced a general practitioner to prescribe Xanax, an antianxiety drug I saw used quite extensively during my internship at the VA hospital in the late 1980s. I took the pills until the day I left Long Island and then I stopped. Although they worked wonderfully and had no noticeable side effects (the most worrisome—reduced libido—was irrelevant to me at that time), I have not since taken such medication.

I returned to Riverdale with a genuine sense of relief, believing I would resume the life left behind when I moved to Long Island. I began working out at the health club, rejoined Achilles, reconnected with Adria, and found new biking partners.

Joan and I resumed our friendship. In the painful days between the time Jamie and I agreed to separate, I reached out to Joan for solace. Although we hadn't spoken since running into each other at a postrace breakfast in 1992, she agreed to have lunch with me and be there if I needed company. I owe her an enormous debt of gratitude for helping me get through a rough period in my life.

During my hiatus from running, I had idealized the athletic life. However, after a few months of trying to resurrect it, I realized I couldn't return to the intensity level I'd left seven years earlier. It was time for a more radical change.

Pressured by a force I couldn't identify, I worked hard at my job and in my exercise routine. Losing all the weight I had gained over the past seven years, I got back into shape. I was spending inordinate amounts of time at work at the Lighthouse including over the past four years, neglecting my marriage. My job was so enveloping and insulating within the walls of the Lighthouse, it threatened to dead-end my career. I had mostly dropped off the professional radar scope of my field. I felt if I didn't do something soon, I would be trapped in my current job forever. Overworked and needing an escape, I decided to look for a new job. As it happened, an opportunity presented itself, and I pursued a position that would require my moving to the San Francisco Bay area.

By coincidence, I had visited Mike in San Francisco in the summer of 1999, about six months before the job offer. We took a few tours, ate at Fisherman's Wharf, spent a day in wine country, and hung out in his Pacific Heights apartment, reminiscing about the glory days. Knowing he was out there and enjoying the few days I had spent in the Bay Area, I accepted the position with the San Francisco office of the American Foundation for the Blind. I moved to Berkeley in January 2000.

The most difficult part of the decision pertained to leaving my family and, once again, Joan. At that time, despite my father's growing list of maladies, my parents were in reasonably good health, and my brothers still lived with them. I felt comfortable that they would take care of each other. Joan and I spent a wonderful New Year's Eve together, hugging and saying goodbye on New Year's Day. The next day, my belongings two weeks behind me in a moving company truck, I boarded a plane for San Francisco.

My new position with the American Foundation for the Blind's National Employment Center promised to be quite fulfilling. I'd gotten acquainted with its director in 1995 at a leadership conference in Washington, DC and met him again a few years later when he visited the Lighthouse. The job seemed perfect for me. It lived up to expectations, exposing me to a national arena, allowing me to write and publish, exercise leadership skills, and pursue projects that matter to a national audience within my field. I was back on the professional radar scope.

In April of 2000, I met Cathy, the woman I've probably been looking for my entire life. A true California girl, exuding a combination of sophistication and trust, Cathy was a professor of history and a disability studies specialist. A UC Berkeley ("Cal") grad, her liberal politics often stretched my slightly more conservative New York sensibilities. We complemented each other nicely right from the beginning.

Cathy seemed to know me better than I knew myself. Introduced by colleagues, after dating for two years, we decided we would be happier living together. We moved into a lovely cottage in Berkeley. She helped me to understand that intimate relationships frightened me and helped me kick the desire to flee.

In March 2000, I added another sports hero picture to my wall. I attended a ceremony in Dallas honoring people improving access to information for the blind. The emcee was Randy White, the Hall of Fame defensive tackle who played with the Dallas Cowboys from 1975 to 1988. I approached the stage after the ceremony and convinced him to take a photo with me by mentioning our mutual acquaintance, Jimmy, with whom I wrestled in high school and with whom he played at the University of Maryland. The photo shows me, with my cane, standing next to and dwarfed by the six-foot-four-inch, 265-pound giant. He gently and affectionately wraps his arm around my shoulders. There I stand proudly, an athlete with a cane, alongside a man who struck fear in all his gridiron opponents. For that moment, Randy White became another in a long list of "guardian angels."

In 2001, tragedy not only struck New York City but Jamie as well. There is irony and sadness in the story.

A year after our divorce, Jamie married her childhood sweetheart, the old boyfriend who had suddenly returned to her life and put the final nail in the coffin of our marriage. She seemed, from all accounts, to be happy, having finally found her lost love.

Jamie and I had mended our relationship enough to feel comfortable keeping in touch by e-mail. Actually, we needed each other; both of us were on protracted debt repayment regimens to extricate ourselves from the financial quagmire we had sunk into during our marriage.

All appeared to be going well in Jamie's life until breast cancer struck. She noticed lumps, went to several doctors, and had a radical mastectomy. It wasn't enough. The cancer metastasized to her brain.

She underwent all the usual therapies, had her driver's license temporarily revoked, recovered sufficiently to get it back, and then got worse again. By early 2002, she succumbed.

I heard about her death from former coworkers. Persona non grata, I did not return to New York to attend the funeral. Instead, I mourned her passing and the failure of our marriage—something I had not yet fully accomplished—in the close comfort of my relationship with Cathy.

On a brighter note, after years of long-distance dating, Mike finally married Diane. They live in Marin County, north of San Francisco and have two beautiful boys. He and I don't talk about the glory days anymore, but for a while, we would allow ourselves to lapse nostalgic from our respective armchairs and contemplate running the Bay to Breakers seven-mile race.

My career movement continued. After five and a half years with the American Foundation for the Blind, another dream job opportunity came my way, and I pursued it.

In 1995, seeing no near-term opportunity to advance to a job in state agency administration, I left government service for the private sector. In the years I spent there, I had learned a great deal. One of the more important lessons, and one I'd instinctively known about since the beginning of my career, is what it is like to be on the receiving end of someone else's exertion of power. As a government official with not only a broad perspective of the market but also the purse strings, I was always careful not to bully the private sector contractors with whom I dealt. "One should use one's strength and power wisely and judiciously." I said this not only to myself, but to everyone whom I'd ever supervised. "Remember," I'd quip, "those you mistreat on the way up will be laughing at you on the way down!"

Unfortunately, not everyone in government service feels this way. Some use their role as fiscal guardians to demand from the private sector more than is fair for the available dollars. I prefer a balanced approach, a partnership, where each side bears its fair share of the burden.

My next career opportunity was born in 2003. A new division (akin to the Commission for the Blind in New York) was established in the Department of Rehabilitation in California. I competed for the leadership position, but lost to an insider. In 2005, she announced her retirement. Encouraged by the hiring manager with whom I'd interviewed the first time to try again, I applied and won the job.

I assumed my duties as lead administrator of the Specialized Services Division in September of 2005. Back in state service, I enjoyed the challenges of facilitating culture change in a sometimes-intractable but also quite potent governmental system. As I consolidated my power, I put into play more fully the philosophy of partnership with private sector agencies for the deaf and blind, the constituency groups my division was charged with serving.

Lessons Learned

It took the unfolding of many years for me to be able to tell this story and to realize that publicly admitting my imperfections might serve as a vehicle of hope to others and not a source of embarrassment for me. To expose them in writing required my developing comfort with (if not grudging acceptance of) those imperfections.

In working out where my blindness figured in this calculus, I believe I have gotten closer to understanding how disability is neither a single, unconnected characteristic nor an unconquerable dominating factor in a person's life. Unfortunately, the general public tends to think in terms of either one or the other of these notions. In fact, both notions are too simplistic.

To fully understand the disability experience, one must accept that it is neither a simple characteristic nor an omnipresent phenomenon. Forced to choose, most disability advocates would rather the public consider disability as simply a characteristic of a person (e.g., "He is a person who happens to be blind."). They promote this image to get the public to treat the disabled with equality and not with pity.

The notion of transcendence is equally simplistic and at best only partly true. It goes like this: "Because he can't see, his hearing and memory have become extraordinary." "Blindness has created in him an appreciation for the world around him most of us never attain." "It forced him to work hard, which built discipline he would not have achieved were he sighted." Finally, "He rose above the experience of blindness, not letting it keep him down, and achieved at a higher level than anyone would have expected."

While blindness does strengthen us if we put forth the effort, the difficulties created by lack of vision can also exacerbate our "imperfections." I'll call this "reverse transcendence." For example, a blind person with average talent and a tendency toward leg injuries may not achieve his full potential as a runner—not for lack of extraordinary will and fortitude, but because he cannot train at precisely his own rate and pace. Similarly, the notion that providing a running partner completely offsets the disabling aspect of blindness is an incomplete one. It is comparable to teaching a child to swim with water wings but not with just his or her arms.

I advocate a more complete approach. The "mere characteristic" approach will hopefully open the door for people with disabilities. This is a necessary first step. However, after the door has been opened and true integration into society has begun to take root, the "transcendence" and "reverse transcendence" elements must be managed. For example, in social situations and at work, proper planning for unforeseen contingencies will create optimal conditions for people with disabilities to reach a fuller potential. It is not enough to say, for example, "Well, we provided the accommodation, shouldn't that be enough?"

The answer is "Usually, not." Things are often unpredictable, and new problems are inevitable. We must allow for new things to crop up as the person attempts their sport or job that may pertain as much to their personhood as to their functionality.

Getting people with disabilities fully into the mainstream of life is a two-step process. First, we must do the right thing. Provide a level playing field and reasonable accommodation to enable, say, a blind person to take a job or join a running club. This step still creates resistance among many in our society. Perhaps the resistance comes from an instinctive knowledge that the next step is inescapable.

The next step requires similar cooperation. We must make sure the individual fares well and flourishes. It is not enough to throw someone into the pool with water wings; we must train the individual to swim and to do so skillfully. In the long run, everybody wins when we remember that the human element requires ongoing attention to yield optimal performance.

Is winning the only thing? In deference to the great Vince Lombardi, my answer is no. Win or lose, since we can't be perfect, I believe our duty is to do the best we can to live as good a life as possible. Coaching is a key not only in how to win but in how to lose—especially without shame. The process begins with good parenting. Parents who provide their children with encouragement and praise, mixed with mild critique when necessary, give them the "stuff" they need to fill themselves with confidence. Participation in organized sports can build confidence. Proper coaching and support can teach youngsters how to work hard to win and how to lose without trauma. These skills transcend sports and affect all aspects of life. Perhaps this is the greatest lesson of all and one that should prompt all parents—including those who have children with disabilities—to push them toward sports and not away from them.

What, you may ask, have I learned about the mental aspect of sports achievement? Regarding my own anxieties during sports performance, I have learned to recognize the symptoms. The sequence for me begins with anxiety followed by a sinking feeling. This has nearly always caused premature fatigue. This is manageable. It requires awareness and strategic planning.

The first step is pacing. Even if it is necessary, it can be frustrating to slow one's self down when he wants to accelerate. However, I have learned that slowing down upon the first signs of fatigue fosters recovery. This is especially true when the end is not in sight. I can generally finish what I start by telling myself that if I relax and stay the course, all will be fine in the end.

Does visual impairment add to the fatigue phenomenon? I believe so, both directly and indirectly. Directly, the added effort required to function and the anxiety that naturally occurs due to partial, confused, or complete lack of visual input adds to energy output. Indirectly, lack of opportunity to compensate makes things worse. For example, in my youth, I probably could have gotten into better shape by doing more running and participating in wrestling camps.

Unfortunately, my parents and coaches did not encourage these activities. With normal vision, I probably would have participated in football in the autumn and baseball or track in the spring, improving my fitness level immeasurably. Had I been able to see the scoreboard or, more important, gotten someone to continually provide me with information, I might have maintained a clearer sense of how much time was left in a period of wrestling or, later, in my running career, the exact location of the finish line in a race. In short, I may have better managed the fatigue with more control of my circumstances, an awareness of what lay immediately ahead, and a more accurate sense of the end of the event.

As much cross-training as I would eventually do as a runner, I could have probably done more. Some difficulties arise when depending upon running and cycling partners. The pace, distances, and frequency of my practices were altered by the need for and presence of other people literally inside my workouts. Indeed, many times, solely because of the availability of a partner and the fear another partner might not be available for days, I would run when a day of rest was in order.

Stationary bicycles, treadmills, other exercise machines, swimming pools with roped lanes, and weight lifting equipment can mitigate a blind athlete's dependency on others. Since to truly build running strength one must hit the road, these ancillary tools can help make the roadwork more consistently constructive.

Part of quality training is learning how to deal with injury and fatigue during a competition. It takes concentrated effort to develop a sense of efficacy about getting past the walls one hits during a grueling athletic endeavor. Hill and sprint workouts help in this regard. I discovered that working out in physical proximity to a partner complicates this process. When your bodily responses become a part of the interaction, it is more difficult to train yourself to vary your pace or learn to privately grin and bear your discomfort. Assertiveness helps. Workout partnerships must be built on mutual respect for the mental and physical welfare of both partners. This means that all aspects of the workout or competition, including fatigue management, are open for discussion.

Fatigue management should be a part of every athlete's coaching regimen as well as a topic for every running and cycling partnership. It is also good to work with partners who are in better physical condition than you. Blind athletes need to know themselves well enough to lead a discussion of strategies to deal with fatigue. Partners can serve as coaches when bouts of fatigue befall a team member during workouts or competitions. For example, when the blind athlete takes the lead and informs his partner he is tired, the partner can say, "Okay, we'll slow our pace until you feel better" or "Concentrate only on your form, relax, and don't worry about the race."

What about anxiety? Competition can raise negative anxiety in those who doubt their ability to win. Those more self-assured feel a healthier (positive) kind of stress, one that galvanizes and energizes them. When fear of losing becomes the dominant factor, it's almost inevitable for one to become a "head case." The secret to avoiding this malady, I believe, lies in helping athletes to develop a sense of control of every aspect of their competitive experience. Attention to the psychological, social, and physiological athlete is a hallmark of great coaching. We should all hope to find great coaches in our lives. They truly make a difference.

My experiences have taught me to pace myself, to plan for extended activity, the long run and sustainability, and how not to "leave my race at the starting line." In my view, since the national trauma of the September 11 attacks in 2001, many people, believing that life is too short and that there is no time like the present, rush too quickly into action. Practice in staying the course under nonideal conditions has enabled me to resist the temptation to go into hyperdrive when slow and steady will win the race.

What would I do if I could do it all over again? It's easy to slide into fantasy. Imagining myself training for a triathlon, I see myself working quite hard, but doing it differently. I mix more sprints into my practices for all three events. I pump a lot more iron. I do not succumb to the temptation to buy the lightest-weight running shoes, no matter how convincing the salesperson is about the latest shock-absorption technology built into them. I cross-train every day to spread the stresses across my entire body. Somehow, becoming faster and stronger, I manage to avoid getting injured.

I plan to live the rest of my life in a more relaxed and well-rounded manner, exercising for the fun of it, controlling my weight, doing the things that make me happy, and, remaining so for a long, long time. No longer a marathon wannabe, I have put that Dustin Hoffman movie away. I reserve the right, however, to succumb to the urging of my sweet tooth whenever it beckons and to pursue personal projects simply because they make me happy. I've never given up my "kid habits"; the Yankees are still my favorite team, and I'll go to great lengths to watch a *Star Trek* show or movie.

As for pursuing a doctorate, my advice to those who ask is to undertake this activity for the right reasons: because it is your heart's desire and because you see a bona fide use for the knowledge and credential after you finish. If I were to pursue a doctorate again, I would try to arrange to do it full-time, pursue its completion with a degree of tenacity and single-mindedness that was absent from my attempt, and hope that the support and love of others will be there to see me through.

Abraham Maslow spoke of the human condition in terms of need fulfillment. He said we must have our basic need for physiological nurturance, safety, and security fulfilled before we can move on to loftier endeavors. Maslow said we are driven toward finding a complete sense of self (esteem) in all we do. The goal is to develop a sense of pride. The ability to hold one's head high—win or lose—numbers among the loftiest achievements in life. Strenuous athletic endeavor certainly has put me in touch with these needs.

While I continue to work at nurturing my sense of esteem, I have turned my attention to the future—toward filling Maslow's highest need—self-actualization. This is the desire to fulfill all possible potentials, to be all that one can be, and to become a complete person.

Toward this end, I believe I have met one of my greatest challenges. I have discovered that the child that I thought I lost the day I first put on a pair of eyeglasses is still within me. I have allowed myself to touch the hand of that child, permitting myself to grieve past losses and to reembrace ideals I thought I'd lost forever. As precious as the moments would have been had I touched the hands of children reaching on to the marathon course in Brooklyn, they could not hold a candle to the experience of touching the hand of the child within.

No longer measuring my sense of well-being solely on what I've accomplished, I now take pride and fulfillment from the journey itself. Staying the course is important. It is better to have a solid .500 record than no record at all.

Resolution

How do we resolve the conflict between the necessary and beneficial drive toward excellence, so deeply ingrained in human culture, and our equally inherent imperfections? Can we ever learn to glory in the loving of the game and keep the pressure to win from spoiling the endeavor? Or has Vince Lombardi's dictum ("Winning isn't everything; it's the only thing") become axiomatic in our society?

Once I heard about an amazing occurrence in the Paralympics. A developmentally delayed young lady, approaching the finish line and well in front in a racing competition, deliberately gave up her chance to win the event. Looking over her shoulder, she noticed a competitor fall to the ground. Instead of racing across the finish line, winning the race, and reveling in her victory or perhaps even returning to check on the athlete, the young lady stopped running, flagged down the other racers, and quickly convinced them to assist their fallen comrade. After helping the fallen racer to his feet, the group walked across the finish line as a single unit. I didn't hear how the judges handled this marvelous act of selflessness. If it were me, I would have awarded the gold, silver, and bronze in accordance with the racers' positions just before the event changed from a competition to a lesson in humanity.

This act of human kindness only served to confuse me more. On the one hand, I appreciated how far, steeped in the culture of excellence, American society has come in a historically short time. After all, someone taught her the values that led to her acting as she did. Say what you may about our occasional bouts of misguided global politics, Americans can be proud of their societal achievements. Unfortunately, the young lady's laudable action also evoked in me the categorical imperative. What would happen to our society if we all acted in competitive situations the way she did? How would humans ever achieve excellence?

To be sure, there are productive and well-adjusted societies in the world much less driven by the need to be on top. One could argue that in their development as powerful nation-states, many of these societies once had their colonial period. Having fallen from power, they have settled down to concerning themselves about the welfare of their own citizenry, preferring to project world power through multinational efforts.

Some say American culture is currently geared for its own brand of colonialism, using its economic power and, occasionally, its military might in the name of liberation to gain economic rather than strictly territorial ends. Most of us feel conflicted by this notion. If this truly reflects our present cultural ethos, one can only hope that our society will someday resolve the issue. To do so, we will need to do something uniquely American: develop a way of life that exults in being the strongest while maintaining respect for those who are not. Such a society judiciously sublimates its interests for the betterment of the entire family of nations. Only a truly strong society can risk humility and deference to those not so fortunate or powerful.

A case in point relates to the protracted argument that took place in the 2000s about what to do with the space that once held the World Trade Center towers in New York City. In the months immediately following September 11, 2001, many people argued for replacing the towers with structures as imposing and power-evoking as the originals. Officials of the City of New York held a contest, receiving designs from scores of architects. The winner proposed to build a functional office building, the "Freedom Tower," which towers as tall as the originals. However, the highest portion of the tower does not carry solid building structure. Gossamer, it recreates the skyline so sorely missed by New Yorkers and reflects light at key points in the year (especially on September 11).

Unfortunately in my view, although the design represents a compromise between power projectors and peace lovers, its failure to totally eschew the expression of power, less necessary to flaunt today than more than forty-five years ago when the original towers were designed and the country feared the might of the Soviet Union, reveals that our society is growing, but not yet fully mature.

Recently I read a prize-winning essay in the NY Times by Avram Alpert. Entitled, "The Good-Enough Life", Mr. Alpert said, "The desire for greatness can be an obstacle to our own potential." He referred to various philosophies ranging from Aristotle, to psychotherapy, to Buddhism, emphasizing those that say that while greatness is sought by many, it is the form in which that greatness takes that can be moderated to include the average person. The tasks may be daunting (like raising a child well), but the accolades small. Alpert posits that most of us, will achieve greatness by having "sufficient (but never too many) resources to handle our encounters with the inevitable sufferings of a world full of chance and complexity."

As humanity evolves, competition and excellence will coexist with compassion and cooperation. When it does, I believe humans, as a race, will achieve the kind of self-actualization Maslow posited for individual beings. Today, sports serve to diffuse our tendency toward violence. In the future, sports will not be needed for this purpose. Our tendencies will evolve to a point where violence will be universally regarded as a truly last resort. When that day comes, sports participation also will have evolved into the truly enjoyable activity the ancient Greeks meant it to be.

There is hope. If we teach our children to follow their competitive instincts without instilling in them a "survivalist" mentality, the athletic experience will become a sought-after and integral part of everyone's life.

In the early 1970s, it was no coincidence that my college campus contained a few champion athletes who, burned out by the end of their high school careers, did not sign up for college sports. The intensity of their practices, a single-minded drive toward athletic excellence, and pressure to win had prematurely robbed them of the enjoyment of sport.

Competition should be encouraged. However, it should be taught as a state of mind as much as a skill-based activity. In a martial arts mentality, for example, children can be taught to strive for superior physical and mental control and maintain peace of mind and drive, even when they don't meet the expectations of either themselves or others.

What about blind children? Several years ago, I attended a business luncheon with an official of the United States Association of Blind Athletes (USABA). We discussed methods for assuring that blind children obtain proper physical education, including basic physical skill instruction, lifetime fitness education, and exposure to both mainstream sports and sports designed for the blind. We would have been gratified to know that a decade and a half later, the blindness professional organization (AER) would form a new Physical Activity and Recreation Division.

"Blind children," he said, "need to be taught how to run, skip, throw, roll, climb, and more. They don't pick up these skills by watching others. At our camps, we teach them to do all these things." Then he said proudly, "I've trained blind children and adults to belay up and down vertical rock faces fifty feet high."

I offered that many blind adults appear to be overweight. They don't seem to know how to stay fit. Admittedly, blind people face many barriers in maintaining effective exercise and dietary regimens. They can't simply jump on a bicycle and go for a joy ride or roll out of bed into a morning jog. Not everyone can afford a stationary or tandem bike; arrangements have to be made for bicycling or running partners. Still, with available transportation, health clubs welcome blind patrons, and personal trainers can provide knowledge and motivation for fitness and weight control.

Healthy eating is easier to accomplish. Plenty of accessible material is now available to learn proper diet management. Blind people can learn effective cooking and other food preparation techniques by taking classes at local centers for the blind or by simply apprenticing themselves to other people, both blind and sighted.

The USABA representative stated, "Many blind people don't know how they could possibly participate in a softball or soccer game with sighted players." He asked me, "What would you tell them?"

I suggested that for softball, batting might be accomplished by hitting from a batting tee. Base running can be done using a fixed sound source or sighted partner. I admitted that sliding might be a challenging problem, but not unsolvable. A sighted partner could time the slide and cue the blind runner at the precise moment. This would require lots of practice. As for fielding, a partner could assist the blind player, and once the ball is retrieved or caught, the blind player can do the throwing.

Blind soccer players might play with a modified soccer ball, one that contains a bell on the inside. A sound-producing device could be placed behind the center of the net to provide audio cues for shots on goal or free kicks.

He continued, "Then there's goal ball and beep softball, two sports designed especially for blind people."

Actually, I have played both sports. Goal ball is played in a gymnasium with a weighted basketball containing a bell. Each team stands on opposite ends of the floor and attempts to roll the ball underhanded past the opponents and across their end line. Goal ball teams contain three players—a center and two wings. A neutral zone lies between each team's portions of the floor. Defenders slide their bodies sideways to present a maximum profile to block the oncoming ball.

Beep baseball uses an oversized softball containing a pulsing beeper and beepers at first base and third base. The pitcher is a member of the offense. He pitches the ball, underhand, into the batter's swinging zone. Fielders are placed at approximately the same defensive positions as regular softball infielders. A "short fielder" is sometimes included. There are no outfielders as it is nearly impossible to hit the heavier softball very far in the air.

If a ball is batted to the left side of the field, the first-base beeper is activated by a line coach. If the ball is batted to the right side, the batter is cued to run to third base. If the batter reaches the base before the ball is picked up or caught by the defense, a home run is scored. If the fielder secures the ball first, an out is registered. In both cases, as soon as the play is over the batter leaves the field. Three strikes (fouls and missed swings) and you're out, three outs and the inning is over; the leader after seven innings wins the game.

What about "regular guys"? Is there a rightful place in the world for average and below-average athletes? Of course. I have heard that in many sports, some of the best coaches were, themselves, only "average athletes." They understand both how to overcome adversity and realize high achievement. When we learn as a culture to look beyond the surface, beyond the hype, we will realize that "ordinariness" is indispensable to the basic functioning of society. Indeed, if we remember that mathematically, the average is the sum of the highs and the lows, all divided by the whole, we will learn neither to overly flaunt our excellent traits nor to undersell ourselves because of our shortcomings. After all, the combination of our attributes makes us what we are—beings greater than the sum of our parts.

Conclusion

I have learned that it is possible to accept one's situation without succumbing to fatalism. Our lives are like a woven tapestry whose threads connect our past to our present. We are the sum of all that has come before us. Yet we are not bound by our past, only influenced by it. We can change the direction of the weave. By taking our fortunes and misfortunes and creating a foundation out of them, we can look ahead, not back. We can flourish where we've never flourished before. The game is not fixed. As we change and approach the game differently, so too shall the game change for us. Whether we decide to stand up or sit out, the past is the past and the future is always in front of us.

Epilogue

My friend and I circle the track at what seems to be an accelerated pace. The children leave the soccer field, the game has just concluded. They gather together on the sideline and have a group hug. The hard-fought competition has ended with a few bruised knees, some injured egos, and lots of fraternity.

"That's the way to play the game," I comment. I notice I am breathing a little harder from greater-than-usual exertion. It feels good. As a matter of fact, everything has felt better since I began regularly doing calisthenics, running, stationary biking, swimming, and road cycling on my tandem. Push-ups, sit-ups, some dumbbell work, and lots of stretching have made my body feel tight and strong again. I have joined early morning spin classes at the local health club. Spreading the body stresses across muscle and bone groups as well as over time is proving a winning formula.

My friend catches her breath. She observes, "It looks like they played a hard game."

We complete our run, and I check my watch. "Wow!" I exclaim. "No wonder we're out of breath. We did that mile in ten minutes. You're getting faster."

"I'm tired of the same old eleven-minute runs," she declares. "It's time to step it up a notch."

I think, "Now we're cooking! As soon as we break the nine-minute mark, I'm joining the local running club." I see it now. My mileage and speed increase, my cross-training regimen accelerates, and before I know it, I'll be ready for the Bay to Breakers race, or even the four-hundred-mile AIDS ride. Fear not, dear reader; I took it just a little easier than that!

Time Moves On

People seek their happiness. In 2008, Cathy and I decided to live apart, and I moved to Sacramento to be near my job. The on-and-off arrangement we had with my living part-time in Davis and part-time in Berkeley wore thin, and after a while, we decided to revert to a close friendship which, we maintain to this very day.

In late 2008, my father succumbed to a multitude of illnesses and passed away. My brothers look after my mother. I eventually met a new lady, and we gamely undertook a long-distance relationship when, in 2010, I accepted a job in Southern California that would be the capstone of my career. I directed the opening of a new blind rehabilitation facility inside the Long Beach VA medical center.

After five years, the organization was mature. Single again, I am not built for sustained long-distance relationships, I took early retirement and returned to my native New York.

In New York, I live in my dear Riverdale which has remained relatively stable over the years. I enjoy a moderate exercise routine, part-time employment, and a well-balanced leisure life. The future indeed is always in front of us. Time will tell what will come next.

Coda

I wrote these memories and musings of a blind wrestler, runner and all-around regular guy to make sense of my life and transmit my discoveries to others. I chose to focus on my athletic career because it presented the most fun filled and understandable way for me and (I hope) others to understand my discoveries. The most important of these is the basic task of all of us to find harmony between our fundamental imperfections and the demands upon us for high performance. Except for the very few at the extremes, most of us reside at the peak of the normal curve. We are regular guys (and gals). Thus, we strive through life pitting our imperfections against our assets. Life ends up being a blend of both of these.

It is my fondest hope that these pages have informed the reader about how various sports and athletic endeavors take place from the inside out. I chose to talk most about the sports I know best: wrestling and running, to a lesser extent skiing, swimming, scuba diving, and my beloved baseball, and a few in which I only dabbled.

Finally, I hope that the reader has gained a keener understanding about the relationship between that which is considered "normal" and that which is not. We go through life with a small set of skills and a larger set of imperfections, all of which must reconcile for us to have a complete and coherent life.

Mine began as the object of the high hopes of two very young parents whose generation lived through a Great Depression and a World War. My visual impairment not only threw a monkey wrench into their lives, it threw an even bigger one into mine. This regular guy was assigned the daunting task of doing the best he could to grow up, work and play hard, and make something of his life. Adding to the challenge was continual loss of eyesight and the battle to fight against increasing disability or die trying. Coming to grips over and over again with encroaching blindness made me stronger and more resourceful, but it also left me more fatigued and prone to anxiety.

The glory of it all lies in love's labor's lost: bodily integrity found then lost and then found again; relationships also found then lost and then found again; career decisions requiring me to uproot myself numerous times and lose relationships in the process, to expend a great deal of energy and to come out the other end smarter and more experienced; and, oh yes, let us not forget the trials and tribulations of life that all of us experience, including those of us with disabilities.

Thank goodness for sports. We have been a good fit. Whether I stood up or sat out, I have no regrets. I love being physical. Sports were—and remain—the glue that has held me together.

References

Achilles International (2017). Available: https://www.achillesinternational.org/.

A. Alpert (February 20, 2019). "Opinion | The Good-Enough Life." *The New York Times.* Available: https://www.nytimes.com/2019/02/20/opinion/the-good-enough-life-philosophy.html?fallback=0&recId=1IJ3PuAz4W5vBYQ9J8S6Dgo22U3&locked=0&geoContinent=NA&geoRegion=NY&recAlloc=home-desks&geoCountry=US&blockId=home-living-vi&imp_id=440018913&action=click&module=Smarter%20Living&pgtype=Homepage

Astoria, NY (2006–2012). Available: http://www.astoria.org/ (Available on line: http://www.sitebits.com/newyork/astoria/).

B. Dellinger (2011). The oldest sport. (National Wrestling Hall of Fame). Available on line: http://nwhof.org/stillwater/resources-library/history/the-oldest-sport/.

R. Francis. (2001). "Two Wrestlers." In N. Blaustein (ed.). (2001). *American Sports Poems.* Iowa City: University of Iowa Press, 86.

R. Hayden (2001). "The Diver." In N. Blaustein (ed.), (2001), *American Sports Poems.* Iowa City: University of Iowa Press, 114.

R. Hellickson and A. Baggot (1987). *An Instructional Guide to Amateur Wrestling.* New York, Putnam.

J. Kempton. (April 1992). "Candela coming home to run HHH Classic 10K race." *Rockland Journal News*, Available: https://lohud.newspapers.com/.

Marathon Man. (1976). (Available on line: hht[://www.rottentomatoes.com/in/Marathon Man _1013283/reviews.php).

Marathon Man. (2019). Marathon Man (Film). Available: https://en.wikipedia.org/wiki/Marathon_Man_(film)

D. Martin (August 26, 1989). "Reject All Limits: A Blind Athlete Competes Boldly." *New York Times*, p.25.

Central Park Triathlon-New York Triathlon (2017). Available: https://nytri.org/central-park-triathlon/.

A. Rodriguez and C Black (1997). *The Tandem Book*. Lake Forest, CA. Info Net Publishing.

Smithsonian Institution (2017). The Steinway Family and Steinway and Steinway Sons: The William Steinway Diary: 1861–1896. Available: http://americanhistory.si.edu/steinwaydiary/annotations/?annotation=117.

W. Stafford (2001). "Run Before Dawn." In N. Blaustein (ed.). (2001). *American Sports Poems*. Iowa City: University of Iowa Press, 207.

P.G. Stoltz & E. Weihenmayer (2006). *The Adversity Advantage: Turning Everyday Struggles into Everyday Greatness*. Touchstone: New York.

Tarrytown, NY (2007). *A Brief History of Tarrytown*. Available: http://www.tarrytowngov.com/about-tarrytown/pages/a-brief-history-of-tarrytown.

"The Third Annual National Hero Awards (August 12, 1991)." *People* magazine, p.26. Available: http://backissues.com/issue/People-August-12-1991.

R. Traun and M. Calizio (1993). *A Victory for Humanity*. Waco, TX, WRS Publishing.

USA Track and Field (Long-Distance Running). Available: http://www.usatf.org/Sports/Road-Running/LDR-Division.aspx.

US Association of Blind Athletes. Available: https://www.google.com/search?hl=en&source=hp&q=US+association+of+blind+athletes&oq=US+association+of+blind+athletes&gs_l=psy-ab.3..0.1154.8311.0.8325.32.26.0.0.0.0.333.3482.0j12j5j1.18.0....0...1.1.64.psy-ab..14.18.3478...0i131k-1j0i131i46k1j46i131k1j0i22i30k1.zJpGvXclCvw.

E. Weihenmayer (2002). *Touch the Top of the World: A Blind Man's Journey to Climb Farther Than the Eye can See*, Plume: New York.

E. Weihenmayer (2017). *No Barriers: A Blind Man's Journey to Kayak the Grand Canyon*, St. Martin's Press: New York.

R. Wilbur. "Running." in N. Blaustein (ed.). (2001). *American Sports Poems*. Iowa City: University of Iowa Press, 221.

Wrestling History. Available: http://www.collegesportsscholarships.com/history-wrestling.htm.

About the Author

Except for 15 years in California, Anthony Candela is a life-time New Yorker. He worked for more than 40 years as a rehabilitation professional, finishing his career by opening a blind rehabilitation center for the VA in Long Beach, California. Born with a severe visual impairment, he went to school and then to work; competed in sports; loved and lost and loved again; and did all this while slowly going blind. Currently semi-retired, Mr. Candela remains active in enhancing the success of blind persons in the mainstream of life.

Mr. Candela is a "retired" athlete (wrestler and long distance runner). Still an all-around regular guy, he loves movies, sports, reading, writing, and music, dabbling in guitar. The adrenalin rush is never far away, so he still works out whenever he can, thinking about the glory days. He believes winning isn't the only thing; the challenge, camaraderie, and competition count for more. Mr. Candela has faith we will sustain ourselves as a race if we truly recognize the humanity in all of us. People with disabilities can show us the way.